Running A One-Person Business

Running
A One-Person
Business

Claude Whitmyer, Salli Rasberry
and Michael Phillips

Ten Speed Press
Berkeley, California

10

TEN SPEED PRESS
P.O. Box 7123
Berkeley, California 94707

Book Design by David Charlsen
Cover Design by Fifth Street Design Associates
Illustrations by Matthew Wilson
Composition by Recorder Typesetting Network

Library of Congress Cataloging-in-Publication Data

Whitmyer, Claude.
  Running a one-person business.

  Includes index.
  1. Self-employed.   2. Small business—Management.
I. Rasberry, Salli.   II. Phillips, Michael, 1938-
III. Title.
HD8036.W45   1989   658'.041   88-2104
ISBN 0-89815-237-2

Printed in the United States of America
        5 - 93 92

TABLE OF CONTENTS

Other Books by Phillips and Rasberry:

The Seven Laws of Money (New York: Random House, 1974).
The Briarpatch Book (San Francisco: New Glide, 1978).
Honest Business (New York: Random House, 1982).
Marketing Without Advertising (Berkeley: Nolo Press, 1987).

About the Authors

For the last fifteen years Michael, Salli, and I have been privileged to be part of the growing community of one-person businesses from around the world. We have been lucky enough to visit several hundred one-person businesses in Brazil, England, Canada, France, Japan, Sweden, and throughout the United States. Many have called upon us in Northern California from as far as Argentina, Australia, Kenya, New Zealand, South Africa, and Uganda.

It is clear to us that the one-person business phenomenon is worldwide and growing, and there is much to learn and share about what works and what doesn't for this new business form.

The one-person business today is very much a product of our so-called information age. Each of us has learned to manage information in ways that made this book possible. Michael's background in banking and foundation management, Salli's experience in writing, publishing, and managing small businesses, both for profit and nonprofit, and my expertise in computers and management automation made us the best team to present this material in a form that is both detailed and practical.

If you would like to respond to what you read here, ask any questions, or keep abreast of changing developments in the one-person business arena, please feel free to contact us in care of: The Enterprise Support Center, P.O. Box 77086, San Francisco, CA 94107.

—CW

ACKNOWLEDGMENTS

George Young, the publisher of this book, said I could have a whole page of my very own. This pleases me very much. It pleases me because it's time to be me instead of we. I want to say right off that if you think, as I once did, that writing a book with two other people makes the whole process easier, it doesn't. It does have its rewards, however, and we learned an incredible amount from one another. Thanks, Michael and Claude, for sharing the experience of making this book. I love you both.

I am the kind of person who reads every name in the acknowledgments. I'm a romantic, and often the author's expression of love and downright gratitude touches me to tears. I know how important many people were to us and hope I have remembered to thank each of you personally, as well as in print. Thanks to you who rubbed our backs, cooked us dinner, critiqued the manuscript, let us interview you, or offered words of cheer when we felt low. I would especially like to acknowledge the support and encouragement of Michael Eschenbach, Dennis Gillman, Fran Peavey, Tom Hargadon, Gordon Grabe, and Gail Grimes. Jim Sullivan, Reuben Weinzveg, Delia Moon, and Padi Selwyn patiently read the manuscript, made helpful changes, and challenged us when they disagreed. Sasha Griffin, my daughter, took on the tedious job of transcribing the interviews; thanks, sweetheart.

George Young was the perfect publisher. He never nagged, was consistently cheerful and supportive. He not only provided us with an excellent editor and designer, he was always there for us. What a treasure.

It takes a good deal of skill and a lot of diplomacy to help others communicate their ideas and passions, strategies and experience. Thanks to Carol Henderson and Sal Glynn, editors *extraordinaire*.

I have had the pleasure of working with David Charlsen for many years and am honored that he was chosen to design our book. He is not only one of the best designers in the business, he is the dearest of friends.

I got to conduct the interviews for this book and was deeply touched by the deep concern for the environment and the commitment to community expressed by everyone I spoke with. Each person was generous in sharing their business experiences; many shared their homes. I treasure the memory of an evening with Bear Kamaroff and his family, the sweet guitar music of Alicia Bay Laurel, the incredible watercolors of Pam Glasscock. Each interview was important. Thanks to Bill Dale, Paul Terry, Kate Bishop, Alicia Bay Laurel, Bear Kamaroff, Malcolm Ponder, Pam Glasscock, Tom Ferguson, Bill Morehouse, Eileen Mulligan, Catherine Campbell, Norman Prince, Alexandra Hart, Nadine Travinsky, Clifford Burke, Teri Joe Wheeler, Suzanne Maxson, Sherri Brautigan, Bob Wachtel, Ted Rabinowitsh, Diane Stuart, Davida Milborn, Lydie Van Gelder, Sharon Cahn, and Catherine Osterbye.

Running A One-Person Business

Introduction—
Business As Lifestyle

For those who feel life is more than making money, the one-person business is an exciting business form. It is business as lifestyle—business as a statement about who you are and what you value.

Many of you are tired of living for the weekend, for two weeks' vacation with pay, and for the promise of the good life when you retire. This book is for those of you who are daydreaming about the possibility of running a sole proprietorship, those of you who are knee-deep in the first year of being your own boss, and those of you who are old hands at it but need specifics and refinement to help you stay a one-person business. This book is for all of you who suspect, or already know, that you can create meaningful work that parallels all that is important in your life.

One of the most fascinating aspects of the one-person business family is the incredible range of lifestyles and goals it embraces. While some of you want a lot of money, to give you toys and a kind of security, others prefer few possessions and a simple lifestyle. Some of you work only to make a living; others view work itself as a positive value. And some of you believe money can buy a lifestyle, while others believe success is defined by living your lifestyle. Whatever you prefer, it can be supported by running a one-person business

From the owners of one-person businesses we often hear what the majority of our business students and clients have said for years: They don't want their businesses to grow large, and they are not interested in becoming wealthy. Norman Prince, a free-lance photographer and long-time colleague, sums up this attitude well: "My business is a service. Providing that service means being friendly, personable, reliable, and responsible. I feel good about my clients enabling me to earn a living doing what I want to do. I've never gotten rich and probably never will. But I like what I do and try to do it well. I let people know how I can help them solve their problems and be of value. It's a symbiotic kind of thing where they are benefiting me by helping me earn a living, and I am benefiting them by giving them a quality product and personal service that is prompt and on target. What more could I want from my business?"

Historically, individual business owners have provided the foundation upon which our system of private enterprise was built. Yet self-employment became a lost art as people began to depend on others for their livelihood. Despite a professed aversion to bureaucrats and gray-flannel suits, the clear choice of most Americans was joining a corporation. By 1970 less than seven percent of the population was self-employed.

But the one-person business has become the new boom industry of the 1980s, particularly small businesses run from the home. An economic reorganization is afoot, and it's just getting started. *INC.* magazine cites a recent study prepared by the Massachusetts Institute of Technology that states, "Between 1978 and 1980, for the first time in the United States, self-employment grew at a faster rate than wage and salary-paying jobs." And in 1985, according to the same study, ". . . 300,000 individuals took up self-employment." In 1986 the Small Business Administration estimated that there were 1.4 million start-ups. According to the American Home Business Association there are 13 million home-based businesses, representing eleven percent of the U.S. work force. And these figures do not include one-person businesses that have an office outside of the home.

People who brave the uncharted world of the one-person business are looking for a greater degree of personal working autonomy than is possible within other career structures. They start one-person businesses for a variety of reasons, but at the top of the list is the desire to be their own boss, without the responsibility of overseeing others. This in turn offers them the opportunity of structuring their lives in creative ways and at the same time better serving their clients.

Who are the people behind the statistics of the one-person business boom? According to the Small Business Administration, more and more women are likely to start their own businesses. In 1982 the U.S. Census Bureau reported that women owned nearly one-quarter of all small businesses with many opting for the efficiency, ease, and satisfaction of one-person businesses. The IRS reported that between 1980 and 1984 the number of female-owned sole proprietorships increased by thirty-three percent. Of the tens of millions of women who have entered the labor force in the last twenty years, many have children and want to be able to spend more time with them, and this is probably the main reason for the increased number of women running businesses from home. Also, it is still not as easy for women to climb the corporate ladder. Many have therefore decided that running their own businesses offers a lot more real security.

Then there are the young people who were social activists in the 1970s and who no longer want to work for big corporations. They are not afraid of taking risks, and they are not loyal to the corporate structure. They also don't believe that business must keep expanding just for the sake of growth or greater riches. Instead they are opting for the freedom, independence, and peace of mind of being their own boss.

Service industries represent another great source of one-person businesses. The vast majority of the labor force is made up of the more than 78 million people who work in the service sector. Although the service industry dominates the economy, many of these jobs are low paying and unfulfilling. Because service businesses are amenable to small-scale operations, people can easily start them on their own. They will probably fare better economically, and they will certainly gain a great deal of fulfillment.

The one-person business has distinct characteristics that make it very different from other businesses. Most business schools have treated the one-person business as a stunted version of regular business, suitable only for gaining experience on the way to a bigger enterprise. This attitude misses the point that many people prefer this unique form of business. For the last ten years, we have had the privilege of advising and teaching several hundred one-person businesses in different parts of the world. When these clients or students asked us for books that spoke to their needs as one-person business owners, we couldn't help them. There just weren't any such books. The only information was in publications aimed at the hobbyist or the small business owner with employees. We found many books about starting a business and a few about running specific types of home businesses, but not one comprehensive book dealing with how to run a one-person business. Nor is there anything available that addresses the importance of this form of business. We decided to fill the void with a very practical book liberally sprinkled with inspiration.

To write this book, we felt it would be valuable to conduct in-depth interviews to supplement our many years of consulting with and teaching one-person businesses. The interviews gave us the chance to delve into the systems that these businesses, many of them run by personal friends, had worked out over the years. Like all the one-person businesses we have known, these are run by unique individuals, whose incomes vary considerably, as do their goals and lifestyles. They represent a variety of fields, and most live in different parts of the United States. One interviewee lives in Scotland. In our discussions, we captured many insights about the real meaning of success and how social issues were of concern.

Although we wrote this book primarily as a practical guide, we also wanted to instill confidence and offer inspiration. It seemed to us that all really good books give the reader confidence—a sense of "I know that" or "I was on the right track" and "I am not alone." We don't deny the fragility of one-person businesses.

Instead we suggest many ways to reduce the inherent risks, drawn from our own experience and from that of the one-person businesses we interviewed. Our hope is that this book will allow you to run your one-person business in an efficient, profitable way while remaining true to your social and ethical values.

This book is about the difference between just making a living as an individual and running a one-person business. This difference shows up in the diligent use of effective record keeping systems, regular activity measurements, and careful planning of daily work strategy. The principles of business are applied to the practices of one person as a sole proprietor. You can do this poorly or brilliantly, and you can use ordinary business measurements to judge your success.

It's a wonderful feeling to arise each day full of passion and zest for the work ahead. It's also exciting to know you are part of a growing group of businesses that can be a positive social force. You can't be fired, and once you've learned to make your business work, you can be secure enough to take strong moral, ethical, political, and environmental stands if you choose. Running a one-person business can give your personal life more meaning. It can also give your social and civic life a level of vitality that working for someone else usually can't deliver.

One

One-Person Business Owners—
A Unique Group

One-person businesses can be found nearly everywhere, and they earn a wide range of incomes. Consider the oil traders who buy and sell drilling rights worldwide and deal in millions of dollars from their home phone. Or the arbitragers and bond dealers working on investment portfolios of their own, with just a telephone and a rented desk in the back of some brokerage office. These one-person businesses are often major forces in the financial market.

In the political realm, a lobbyist in Washington, D.C., and a private consultant specializing in policy analysis are among the best paid and most influential people in our nation's capital. Both run quiet, behind-the-scenes, one-person businesses.

Some one-person businesses are retailers, for instance, the flower shops, juice bars, and shoe repair stores that flourish in many cities. There is a fellow in Seattle, Washington, who motors his little boat around Lake Union selling espresso and croissants to houseboats, ships at anchor, and shoreline offices. Nadine Travinsky in Bodega Bay, California, runs a homey gift and taffy shop that caters to the many tourists who drive through her town year-round.

Traditionally, many service trades are run as one-person businesses, including housekeeping, beauty salons, tailoring, plumbing, carpentry, and mechanics.

There are also the professionals such as realtors, consultants, accountants, and tax preparers.

Regardless of the field, it takes a certain turn of mind, some unique skills, and a big dollop of realism to successfully run a business on your own. As we said earlier, a one-person business is not primarily a stepping-stone to a bigger enterprise, though you could use it in that way. People run one-person businesses because they prefer that form of business. They like the opportunities it gives them—to lead more flexible and expansive personal lives, and to play a larger role in their communities. In this chapter we will talk about the personal attributes, market perspective, and cooperative effort needed to create and sustain a one-person business. Then we will introduce eight people who are running successful one-person businesses, each in a different field.

REQUIREMENTS FOR SUCCESS

Three factors are essential to the success of a one-person business: tradeskill, market focus, and cooperation.

Tradeskill

Popular business magazines often carry glitzy profiles of real-life businesses that read like fairy tales—success stories that shrink years of work into "started making cookies in her trailer and ended up with a multimillion-dollar business." The emphasis is on making a pile of money, being in the right place at the right time, and "If you work hard and have a great idea, you too could be one of the people in these articles." The skill it takes to run a business remains a mystery.

Creating a one-person business and keeping it going involves what we call *tradeskill*. This is a term we had to make up to describe a whole cluster of behavioral attributes that are vital to running a business. Most of these, if you have them, you learned when you were young. You picked up the skills from your parents or from someone else you spent a lot of time with who was in business. Tradeskill is like riding a bike, ice skating, and being lovable: much easier to learn when you're young.

Put bluntly, some people are good at business and others aren't. Either you got it or you ain't. You can go to the most prestigious business school in the country and you won't find anyone talking about tradeskill. So what do you do if you really want to run your own business and you don't have tradeskill? The best approach is to work closely with someone who does have tradeskill for a number of years, slowly assuming more and more responsibility. Do this rather than just jumping in, because in a one-person business there is no partner to pick up the slack and no whiz-bang employees either. There's just you. Being successful in business is not an inalienable right bestowed at birth on every United States citizen. It's actually more like raising a child and getting married. While everyone feels they can do it, few actually know what "it" is. It is beyond this book to deal with marriage and child-rearing. But the fact is that not everyone can start a one-person business and expect to succeed. It's also all right to try, but fail, as long as you have not jeopardized your home or borrowed heavily from your in-laws. It seems best to take a good look and decide if you have the skills, and if not, to become a paid apprentice until you do. It's usually more fun to succeed than fail. Even having parents who were in business for themselves does not guarantee tradeskill.

How do you know if you have it or not? In *Honest Business* (Michael Phillips and Salli Rasberry, Random House, New York, 1981) we identified four attributes that together give you tradeskill:

- Being persistent
- Facing the facts
- Minimizing risks
- Being a hands-on learner

Being Persistent *Honest Business* said:

> The persistence attribute seems to lead to an awareness of the slow process by which things occur in the world and to the realization that time increases the likelihood of success.

Persistence is the ability to push ahead. You have persistence if it's four in the morning, yet you are determined to finish those frames for tomorrow's gallery opening. You have persistence if you finish that landscaping job even though it's seven-thirty on a drizzly evening and you long for a bath and a hot brandy. And being persistent also means having what it takes to plug away a little bit at a time, day after day, until the job is done. The people who succeed in running a business all have this ability to "hang in there" long after others would have given up. Successful business people are not easily pulled off course, nor diverted from those inevitable long, hard parts of running a business.

Facing the Facts Again, from *Honest Business:*

> Being willing to let go is of course what facing the facts is about. It involves the ability to learn constantly from empirical evidence and the willingness to change your behavior when the weight of the evidence tells you to change. This aspect of tradeskill is different from the quality in people that leads them to change their behavior because of new ideas, convincing arguments, pride or whim.

Facing the facts means having the ability to change your behavior when your personal patterns and beliefs are not working for you. It means having the expectation that better decision-making information comes with time. People who face the facts understand that wisdom is gained by the constant re-evaluation of life experiences. If you love white asters and keep featuring them in your landscape design, despite the feedback that clients don't like them, you are not facing the facts.

Minimizing the Risk Business people who minimize risk know that, over time, random activities have an average value and that decisions based on an average are far more reliable than ones based on chance or on a single event. Such perceptions honed into a day-to-day practice are, in themselves, a successful strategy for dealing with business. *Honest Business* put it this way:

> When looking at new businesses most tradeskill people we've known were very open about looking at completely new ideas and strategies, but when the implementation period came, they methodically went about reducing the risk. They find fall-back plans and alternative solutions in the event the main thrust of their venture doesn't work. They constantly think of alternative uses for the equipment they are using, or for subletting their location if their plans don't work.

Being a Hands-On Learner People with tradeskill gain confidence in their decision making by participating in the total process. As *Honest Business* said:

> People who succeed in starting and running small businesses have the hands-on attribute very visibly before they start a business. They learn by touching and doing.

Most people we know with tradeskill like to do their own books, and they pay daily attention to financial material. This tendency seems to be a direct result of the hands-on learning attribute, since the books give a hands-on, comprehensive feeling of the business.

Market Focus

Market focus means finding and focusing on your appropriate market niche. Fortunately, the number of market niches for a one-person business is many times larger than for other business forms. This is so because consumers are becoming much more sophisticated. Greater consumer awareness is leading to an increase in businesses that match goods and services to the consumers who need them. Instead of mass-produced items and generalized services, there is a move toward products and services that are more suited to individual wants and needs.

A particularly interesting example of a one-person business fitting this description is auto brokering. Auto brokers are individuals who will buy your car for you. You specify your budget and the features you are looking for. The auto broker shops for you, gets you the best deal, and delivers to you a car complete with insurance and registration.

Other examples can be found in the food industry. Increased awareness of nutritional needs and the broader availability of specialized cooking utensils and specialty restaurants has led to a demand for cookbooks, cooking newsletters, cooking classes, food delivery services, caterers, and so forth. A delivery service, Waiters On Wheels, has printed up its own menus listing particular items from about thirty local restaurants. You call Waiters On Wheels to place your order. They pick up from the restaurant and deliver to your door the feast of your choice.

Still other examples of market-focused one-person businesses include helping people select, install, and learn to use a wide variety of appliances, such as computers, VCRs, or microwave ovens. Consultants, newsletters, and classes abound on subjects ranging from environmental toxins to sports training regimes.

Less obvious but equally viable market niches can be found in more traditional occupations. Chiropractors, massage professionals, homecare nurses, plumbers, gardeners, painters, professional house-sitters—all can offer some unique approach or a specialized service in their field.

And of course, each of these special service or product businesses needs the support of accountants, lawyers, graphic artists, printers, photocopy stores, word processors, researchers, and others who cater to one-person businesses.

Cooperation

In our traditions, business has often tended to be selfish, cutthroat, secretive, and warlike in its competitiveness. Such behavior can come across as a form of social Darwinism in which survival of the fittest has some ultimate social good. But businesses of all sizes are coming to regard this kind of competitiveness as part of a dying paradigm. It doesn't feel good, it uses up a lot of energy to view the world as hostile, and, possibly most relevant, it isn't efficient.

Cooperation, on the other hand, is a healthy force in the marketplace. The logic is straightforward: By being cooperative you get more help from everyone in every form. The benefits that smaller businesses reap from helping each other are most evident in the widespread formation of referral services for professionals and for health care providers now commonly listed in phone books across the country. Such businesses recognize that helping others in their field get clients helps individual practitioners as well. The same is true for the use of continuing education supported by more and more fields of business.

Cooperation is an essential ingredient for the success of a one-person business. If you do not create or find yourself in a community of other one-person businesses, you will find it extremely difficult to make it in the long haul. One-person businesses thrive in the company of other one-person businesses to whom they can turn for emotional support or whom they can hire as suppliers or subcontractors.

PROFILES OF SUCCESSFUL ONE-PERSON BUSINESSES

Of the twenty people we interviewed to write this book, we chose eight to profile. We did this not because our profile subjects were more successful or more erudite than the others but because they represented the broadest range of locations and fields. Like all the one-person business owners we have come across, these eight individuals are unique. All have defined success in their own terms, and have figured out how to live their lives in their own styles. On the other hand, they live rather ordinary lives. Another consistent trait is that all are committed to their communities and strive to provide them with quality goods and services. All have perseverance as well. In our opinion, these eight people are representative of one-person businesses everywhere. You can learn a lot from them, especially that it is possible to create the meaningful work that you are good at, and to make a living doing it.

Tom Ferguson, MD, Writer, Publisher

When Tom started *Medical Self Care* as a one-person business, he did everything from opening the mail and corresponding with subscribers to dealing with printers and advertisers. Eventually the magazine grew too big and complex for one person. Tom decided to hire others to help him do the parts of the business that he was either not particularly good at or not interested in. Tom's role evolved into doing the things he likes to do, and *Medical Self Care* is currently a part-time involvement.

By training Tom is a physician and by practice a writer and lecturer. The central thread of his work deals with the self-care approach to health. According to Tom, "I went through medical school and decided that I was not entirely enthralled with the exclusively professional orientation of most of the health care system. Having had contact and experience with the folks who put out the *Whole Earth Catalog*, I got very interested in applying their self-sufficiency paradigm to medicine. And since medical school I have focused full-time on helping people to take care of themselves, rather than taking care of them myself."

Tom writes books (*Medical Self Care: Access to Health Tools*, *The People's Book of Medical Tests*, and *The Smoker's Book of Health*) and articles that provide people with information and resources. He also conducts teaching and training workshops and seminars for health professionals in an effort to expose them to a "new way of looking at the health care system in which the central person is not the physician but the individual."

Dr. Ferguson provides free services to the community of health professionals. "I believe that health care is changing," he says. "We are moving away from an old system built around the physician to a new system built around the layperson. I feel I have a special mission to bring this word to health professionals. So I do free consulting and speaking, particularly with medical and nursing students, as well as people in training to be medical professionals. I used to do a lot more writing without being paid, but I really need to get paid for my writing time now. But I'm easy about people reprinting things."

Although his office is only a five-minute drive from the home he shares with his wife in Austin, Texas, for Tom the ideal distance would be about a three-minute walk. "When I was in Inverness, California, working on the magazine," he recalls, "I had that kind of arrangement and it was fun. It meant that I could turn on the phone machine and take a short walk home and not think about the magazine. But if I wanted to stop in for a minute, it was very accessible."

Malcolm Ponder, Accountant

Malcolm's business has evolved over the last ten years from a financial consultancy to tax preparation work for some 235 clients. He works primarily with individual businesses or partnerships, and also assists a couple of small corporations.

Malcolm is Salli's accountant and tries to help her and all his clients keep an eye on their business or personal finances. "I try to do more than just fill out a tax return. In addition to sitting down with my clients to get the information to do the proper tax return, I'm also asking, 'Why are you spending so much in this category?' and 'Let's talk about your overhead and other expenses.' I want to help them with the overall financial part of their business or personal life. Quality is my aim. I try to prepare a totally accurate, perfectly done tax return."

Malcolm strongly believes that community involvement is vital. As he puts it, "Anybody who is in business in any size town ought to be putting a bunch back into the town and community. A by-product is that you get out of it proportionate to what you put in. When I first started my tax preparation business, I was president of the community center in my area and everybody knew I was reliable. When a fund-raising event came around, I took care of the money, which was a relief to the other people because no one else wanted to worry about that aspect. The bulk of any one-person business clientele comes from your community base. So not only do you want to be a major part of that community to help the good things happen, but by being part of that community you'll become known and people will grow to trust you."

A former wholesale banker for Bank of America, Malcolm lent money to corporations and wealthy individuals. He got hired away by a mining and shipping company and was their assistant treasurer for four years. During the fourth year he was in Brazil with high officials in his company, Malcolm remembers, "I was the only one that wasn't at least a senior vice-president. I started studying these people at the top, the people whose jobs I wanted in five or ten years. They were away from their families twenty-six weeks a year minimum, and lots of them were drinking heavily and carousing. I came back from that trip to our house in Bolinas, California, and realized I wanted out. My wife had died when my kids were very small, and my housekeeper had been raising them. The kids were getting to know her real well, and I was this guy who came and visited occasionally. So I got out, and have worked out of my home ever since."

Pam Glasscock, Fine Artist

Pam paints flowers in watercolors, slowly and painstakingly creating almost botanical renderings. She sells her work mostly to galleries and through her shows and occasionally from her studios in Soho, New York, and Freestone, California.

Pam comments on her life in two cities: "For doing my work it's not necessary to be in Manhattan, but for selling my work it's probably desirable. Big collections or corporate buys, that kind of business is conducted more on the East Coast. And given the informal way I conduct my business, I have found that opportunities always seem to come up when I am in New York, because there is just more action there. I'm married to a successful painter, Tony King. We have two small children. We choose to live simply, and we structure our lives so we can enjoy our beautiful country home in California and our flat in Soho.

"I grew up in a family that had a strong ideal of making the world better and didn't care too much about money. The important thing was to be a good person and to do quality work. Quality is something I think about every second I am working. When I reach a certain level, I want to go a little further, and I always have that in mind when I start a new painting.

"I went to New York just out of school because I was very serious about being an artist and I was attracted to the galleries and museums. It was the first place I had been where when you said you were an artist, people responded as if you had said you were a brain surgeon. Or better. In many parts of the country the response is more, 'Oh. That's really nice . . . how do you get away with that?'"

Alicia Bay Laurel, Musician

At the age of nineteen, Alicia wrote the best-selling book *Living on the Earth* and authored several more books after that. A long time resident of Maui, Alicia decided about three years ago to launch a new career as a musician. Now she plays the guitar and sings, performing mostly jazz, pop standards, and Hawaiian music. "I play the kind of music people want to hear," Alicia says with a smile, "I learn a lot of famous songs and even if I've played 'The Girl From Ipanema' six thousand times, and one more person begs me to play it, I'll gladly do it and do the best job that I can.

"Some musicians feel that the work I do is a sellout. They say 'You write music. Why don't you play your own songs?' But I'm interested in serving my patrons by giving them what they want. For a wedding, I'll learn particular songs for people, even if I don't like the songs, because I want to provide exactly the service that is wanted. People like to hear songs they're familiar with, the songs they fell in love to. I will play my original music if I have an audience that is attentive to me personally. I'll give them some of me and see what happens. If they really like it I'll play some more. But the kind of music I generally play is like a job that has to be done—it's background music. I'm playing music to provide a pleasant atmosphere for people to eat dinner by or get married to or whatever. A musician who wants to be a rock star singing their own original songs would be very frustrated filling this niche. I don't have any illusions like that so I'm very happy doing this kind of work."

Alicia uses the freedom of her business to donate her musical services when an event or cause comes up in which she strongly believes. "Sometimes I donate the use of my PA system for different musical groups to use. For example, seven kids from the community were selected to go to Moscow to paint a peace mural. I acted as the musical director and stage manager for all of the groups that performed to raise funds to send them. I also performed for free. Not only did it help promote my business, it also gave me a feeling of value within the community."

Paul Terry, Small Business Advisor

Paul's is a one-person business that works with a team of associates including an attorney, a bookkeeper, an accountant, a financial consultant, a financial planner, and a graphics and advertising person. When he needs assistance, he can use these associates as referrals, confident that their work is of the highest quality. They also refer clients to him. In his words, "It's an effective way to stay a one-person business and yet have access to important resources."

Paul describes himself as someone who "helps, facilitates, and advises through a business planning process that includes dealing with marketing strategies, financial projections and statements, and management issues such as personnel and time management." He considers what he does a small business advisory service rather than a management consulting business, because it truly stresses micro- or small business.

Paul shares his San Francisco home with his wife, who is a potter, and their two children. He has set aside two rooms in the basement which he effectively uses for his office. He has these words of wisdom about running a one-person business: "Being successful is not just connected to making a lot of money, it's having an impact through services offered and products sold. The way a business is run is as important as the fruit it bears."

Bernard (Bear) Kamaroff, CPA, Author, Publisher

"Life isn't just earning money. Life is doing what you need and want to do with the world," states Bear. "Earning money should have some real value to the world. I think selling pet rocks is up the wazoo. There should be some use to what you are doing. It ought to be providing someone with something worthwhile and it ought to be quality."

Bear and his wife and two children live "in the middle of nowhere," Laytonville, California. In 1974 he wrote and published *Small-Time Operator: How to start your own small business, keep your books, pay your taxes and stay out of trouble* and he has been selling a yearly updated version to book wholesalers, libraries, bookstores, mail-order distributors, individuals, and schools ever since. According to Bear, "I run my business out of my home, by myself, upstairs at my desk next to the bed." His operation involves a lot of mail and telephone orders but no direct contact or manufacturing because someone else manufactures his books for him. "You don't have to worry about appearances, what road you are on, or accessibility," he says. "If you have a telephone, a mailbox, and access to a UPS truck, you can run this type of business anywhere."

Kate Bishop, Clothes Designer

Kate designs and produces a line of silk dresses, mostly for custom order. In her two-room showroom in Occidental, California, she sees from one to four clients a week. Clients try on samples which are springboards to creating their own garments. According to Kate, "A lot of the time I'm merely a facilitator. The samples show the range of my work. I use very fluid silks and do a certain kind of finishing. My range is fairly narrow and esoteric. If a customer looks at my samples and likes them, chances are I can design something with her. If that doesn't happen then I can't, and at least we had some fun together." Kate constructs her garments in a studio on the same property where she and her family live, about a twenty-minute drive from her showroom.

Kate defines success as freedom. She says, "I like to remember the words of Christopher Marlowe: 'There is only one success—to be able to live your life in your own way.' I feel successful because I can make a living doing the work I like to do. Working for myself, I can set my own schedule, choose the people I want to work with, and live where I want, which is in the country, far from the hysteria of the fashion industry."

Kate has been supporting herself by designing garments for eighteen years. She started out wholesaling to stores and found that many of her accounts didn't pay, which is, sadly, not unusual in her line of work. The overhead she had to cover included salaries for nine seamstresses. Six years ago she decided to keep two retail accounts that paid on time and become a one-person business specializing in custom work. For Kate the transition was very smooth, and one of the best decisions she ever made. "I dress women for the role of 'beautiful woman.' Most women that I know, including myself, spend most of their time in the role of either businesswoman or mother. These are satisfying roles in a lot of ways, but they are distinctly lacking in romance and glamour. So I provide the romance and glamour. When you go out in one of my fancy evening dresses, you don't talk about work or the kids."

Bill Dale, Computer and Training Consultant

Bill's consulting company, WADALE Associates, uses other consultants who specialize in market research, finance, computer-based training, etc. Thanks to these trusted subcontractors, Bill can present his business as larger than one-person, enabling him to handle a wider variety of projects and giving him more credibility with the multinationals that represent his biggest market. WADALE Associates supplies consulting and training services principally to high-tech companies in the computer and information systems marketplace, focusing on strategic issues, management development, sales, and marketing.

As Bill explains, "My training modules are like tailor-made software developed from a set of standard modules. Generally ninety to ninety-five percent is standard, and word processed to fit the client. I do this by picking the relevant modules from my list (I have over thirty-five now), and then editing them by changing names and other details. This cuts down the amount of development needed, and allows me to produce a high quality product tailored to the client for the price of standard training. I win, the client wins!"

Although Bill feels that focusing on quality may decrease performance in the short term, he believes it is a necessary balancing act for the long-term survival of the business. "If you don't do a quality job, your reputation will suffer and you will lose business. It's ultimately self-defeating to cut corners on quality. Consulting and training are intangibles, and if you don't project an image that promises quality, then people will think you can't do the job. This is particularly important before you get to know someone. Quality and high standards of performance go hand in hand. I don't like doing a job unless it is a quality one."

Bill has structured his business around what is important to him. "My wife and I moved from London, where most of my work is, to Troon in Scotland. We did this to improve our quality of life. Troon is on the coast and has excellent schooling, amenities, and family connections. At the same time it has good travel to London."

2

Bookkeeping

Bookkeeping is the most important part of any business. The first business system to put in place is your books. Most people focus on marketing first, but this is a dangerous strategy. Why? Because almost anything you do to promote business will work. And the better you are at promotion the more business you can get. But without smoothly functioning financial and organizational systems in place, the increase in volume can swamp you and put you out of business overnight. The worst possible response would be to provide lower-grade services or products because you are unable to keep up with the demand. So focus on your financial and organizational systems first.

In many thriving one-person businesses the only bookkeeping is a checkbook and a file folder with receipts. In our experience, businesses with such casual bookkeeping practices are usually unable to grow to an efficient size or respond effectively to changes in market demand. They also operate without the elegance and perfection that is readily achievable in a one-person business.

The level of skill needed for bookkeeping in a one-person business is low by any business standards. Although we recommend that you use the simplest method you can, even the simplest requires some thought, care, and attention. In this chapter we talk about basic accounting principles, financial statements, and inventory control—and generally about the importance of doing your own books so that you will truly understand and control your business.

BUSINESS—
A SET OF MEASURABLE EXCHANGES

From its historic meaning of an exchange between friends, neighbors, or tribes, to its modern sense encompassing the interactions of giant corporations and governments, the word *business* expresses the idea of a set of measurable exchanges. Contained within the historical meaning of business is the idea that the exchange that takes place will be mutually beneficial. This idea can still be found in many small businesses, and it is the cornerstone of any successful small business venture. The measure of this benefit is the money (or some other standard of value) that is received and spent in making the exchanges.

Business does not have to include money, although most people have forgotten this and equate the two. Money is the yardstick of business—the measurement tool that indicates how well or how poorly the exchanges are faring. But it is not the only measurement tool, and the emergence of private barter systems in recent years, as well as the continual exchange of goods and services by many businesses and individuals under the table, testify to this fact.

For a one-person business, as for any business, carrying on many such exchanges requires a comprehensive and objective way of measuring success—known as bookkeeping.

Bear Kamaroff, mail-order publisher, is also an accountant. He speaks from experience when he says, "You've got to know bookkeeping well, and it's simple to learn. There is nothing simpler in the world; it just sounds mysterious. Bookkeeping is just keeping track of money coming in and money going out, the money owed you and the money you owe, and how much is in the bank. That's it."

Book designer Clifford Burke concurs and stresses bookkeeping as the best way to eliminate money as a problem. "I'm becoming more committed to having my books in order. Although I refuse to put money as my first priority, I've come to see that the best way to keep it in its proper place is to keep track of it, and that doing this doesn't need to take a lot of time. Good bookkeeping really helps. I believe in getting your books right and keeping them right. It doesn't mean you have to be any different about the way you do anything else. Business is money after all. It's not just for fun, and it's not just for good works in the world. It really is to make a living."

Eileen Mulligan, a landscape gardener, doesn't like keeping books at all, but she understands the importance of it. "I do my own monthly bookkeeping even though I hate it. That way I know how much money is going through my books. At first I didn't know what I was doing, but now my bookkeeping system is pretty clear. It's straightforward enough that I can deal with the IRS, and that is a major consideration. I have an intuitive sense of how much money is coming in and from where. I still look over my records once a month, however, because I must always be on top of how much each client is costing. I resent spending the time on putting all those numbers together and moving papers around and keeping them in files. I sit there and look out the window; it's a nice day and I'd rather be doing something else. But I continue because I feel that organized records and bookkeeping are absolutely essential. They're the one thing that will make a business fail or succeed."

Alexandra Hart, a desktop publisher, keeps thorough records on all aspects of her business, but her systems are quite simple. "I keep careful track through a checkbook system. At the end of the year, I put all my figures into the ledger. I use a simple double entry system. I don't construct a profit/loss statement. When I'm really concerned about how things are changing, I do a simple cash flow chart for the next three months. Then I can see how everything is shifting a little. Redoing the cash flow and seeing how it has changed is really helpful to me.

"I keep records project by project. In many cases I have to estimate costs ahead of time. I note down the client's name, our agreements, my billing quotes, and whether something will be farmed out. I record the dates and places I go and a description of what I do for the hours billed. I record if I spent money on a typesetter, etc. At the end of the job, if I have underestimated, I eat it and get better the next time. If my estimate was off because of the client, then I try to communicate that and change the amount billed.

"I keep six to eight income columns in my double entry system, and I can see that my workshop line has no entries or that my writing line is bringing in more. Once a year I look at what works."

BOOKKEEPING BASICS—MONEY IN, MONEY OUT

In business, your books are the map of your territory. You can wander around in the territory without a map, but you will make much more intelligent management decisions about which way to go if you have a good map.

Single Entry or Double Entry

The two common forms of bookkeeping used by small businesses are single entry and double entry. Most one-person businesses need only single entry bookkeeping. But if your business has a large inventory, such as an import-export company, if you are a manufacturing business with equipment, such as a one-person cosmetics manufacturer, or if you have a number of investors, you should consider a double entry system. It provides arithmetic cross-checking that will keep your investors happy and your own confidence high with respect to the

---

The Importance of Keeping Good Financial Records

Bernard Kamaroff, "Bear" to his friends, is one of our personal heroes. He speaks eloquently on behalf of being a one-person business and does a good job of running one. Because he is an accountant and the author of the best-selling *Small-Time Operator*, we think it is especially useful to quote him on keeping good financial records.

"I keep track of all my expenses on a simple expense ledger. These are broken down by categories that are important to me and my tax return. I keep track of total income, of people who owe me money, of bills I have to pay, and of how much cash there is in the bank account to make sure it's enough. It's very simple bookkeeping. My total bookkeeping takes me in the neighborhood of two days of work a year. Maybe three at the very most.

"I recommend that people do their books as regularly as possible so that paperwork doesn't back up. This is real important. The problem with bookkeeping is that when the paper backs up, it becomes a nightmare. An hour a day or whatever it takes, do it so it won't pile up.

"The most important information I need to know is who owes me money. I keep track of that constantly. I know who owes me money and keep a watch on it because my business involves a lot of direct credit. Many of my customers call on the phone and get thirty-day terms or ninety-day terms or whatever. Some of them pay regularly and some need to be nudged. There are a lot of people who need to be nudged in order for me to get paid. I don't like that, but I've learned to live with it because they are good people and that's just their way of doing business.

"Another reason for looking at my books is to keep track of my inventory. I basically am selling one book so I don't have a lot of products. Since I've been watching sales each month for several years and I know how long it takes to reprint, I know from experience when it's time to reorder.

"People need to find some way of keeping track of their inventory—what they have, what they don't have, when they need to add to it. Some people don't need records, they can do it just by looking around. Some people need very elaborate inventory records, especially if they are manufacturing something or putting a lot of different raw materials together. They need records so they can figure out how much their product really costs to produce. If they don't keep track, they'll wind up not being able to figure out what to sell their product for."

---

figures that your checkbook and cash receipts records generate. Bear Kamaroff explains it this way in *Small-Time Operator*:

> Double entry is a complete bookkeeping system that provides cross checks and automatic balancing of the books, that minimizes errors, and that transforms business bookkeeping from a part-time nuisance into a full-time occupation. In double entry bookkeeping, every transaction requires two separate entries, a "debit" and a "credit." These terms originated in double entry bookkeeping, along with the expression "balancing the books": total debits must equal total credits for the books to be "in balance."

Single entry differs from this by only requiring one entry per transaction. There are no debits or credits to deal with. The trade-offs are that you lose the error checking capability of double entry. But for most one-person businesses the number of transactions is so small that double entry for error checking is just overkill.

Cash Versus Accrual

For either double entry or single entry bookkeeping, there are two methods of keeping track of the cash coming into and going out of your business: cash and accrual.

You are using the cash method of accounting if you make an entry in your books only when you actually receive some income or pay for some expense. You are using the accrual method if you offer your customers or clients credit (that is, the opportunity to receive a product or service and to pay for it later), and you enter that income into your books before you actually get it; or if you buy supplies or inventory on credit and enter the cost into your books before really paying for it. Any business with a physical inventory of products or parts is required by the IRS to use the accrual method to keep track of its inventory. This means counting the inventory on hand at year-end, even if it has not been paid for yet. Aside from this requirement you can choose to use either method, but once you have begun using the accrual method, you cannot go back to the cash method without filing a special application for a change in accounting method that must be approved by the IRS.

Regardless of what the IRS requires, if you are a business that buys and sells a product inventory, you should use the accrual method. Even if you are a professional service business, strongly consider using the accrual method, since it will give you a more accurate picture of the financial condition of your business.

CHART OF ACCOUNTS

In keeping track of financial information, a good place to start is with the questions you need to answer on Schedule C of Form 1040. However, bookkeeping is not just intended to answer questions for the IRS, but to answer your questions too.

The so-called chart of accounts is an organized way to keep track of all the questions you might want to ask yourself about the financial condition of your business. Following is a chart recommended by the American Institute of Certified Public Accountants; you can adapt it for your own use (*see Figure* 2.1). Don't be thrown by the numbers, which are simply meant to help you in making entries in your books. If you like, you can use abbreviations of the actual categories.

It is not as important that you make a chart of accounts as that you make a list of questions. Among these questions might be some as simple as: How much rent do I pay every year? Rent is a question you need to answer for the IRS. But you might have other questions as well: What are my three top sources of income? How much do I spend on my newsletter each issue? How much do the sleeves for my videotape product cost me each month?, and so forth.

You can go back to the original invoices and receipts any time you wish and figure out these answers. It would be much easier, however, if you had made a category in your checkbook, or a column in your check journal, that was labeled "newsletter." You could have created three categories in your income record for your top three sources of income, say, "consulting," "teaching," and "book sales." And in your expense record you could have created a category called "cost of goods sold," breaking it down into "videotape sleeves," "videotapes," and any other costs related directly to the assembling of your videotape products.

Fig. 2.1   Chart of Accounts

Account No.

BALANCE SHEET (Accounts 1 through 500)
ASSETS (1-300)

Cash (1-50)
Petty Cash (Cash on Hand)	11
Cash in Bank — General (Regular Bank Account)	21
Cash in Bank — Payroll (Payroll Bank Account)	31

Receivables From Others (51-100)
Notes Receivable	51
Accounts Receivable — Customers	61
Accounts Receivable — Others	71

Inventories (101-150)
Inventory — Goods for Sale	101
Inventory — Supplies	121

Prepaid Expenses (151-200)
Prepaid Advertising	151
Prepaid Insurance	161
Prepaid Interest	171
Prepaid Rent	181

Property and Equipment (201-250)
Land	201
Buildings	211
Buildings — Allowance for Depreciation	212
Automobiles and Trucks	216
Automobiles and Trucks — Allowance for Depreciation	217
Furniture and Office Equipment	221
Furniture and Office Equipment — Allowance for Depreciation	222
Machinery	226

	Account No.
Machinery — Allowance for Depreciation	227
Tools	231
Tools — Allowance for Depreciation	232
Leasehold Improvements (Rented Property Improvements)	246
Leasehold Improvements — Allowance for Amortization	247

Miscellaneous Assets (251-300)
- Organization Expenses (Business Starting Costs) — 251
- Deposits (Advance Payments) — 261

LIABILITIES (301-450)

Notes and Amounts Payable to Others (301-350)
- Notes Payable — Short Term — 301
- Accounts Payable (Bills Payable) — 311
- Sales Taxes Payable — 321
- FICA Tax Withheld — 331
- Federal Income Taxes Withheld — 332
- State Income Taxes Withheld — 333

Expenses Owed to Others (351-400)
- Accrued Wages (Wages Owed) — 351
- Accrued Commissions (Commissions Owed) — 356
- Accrued Interest (Interest Owed) — 361
- Accrued Federal Unemployment Taxes (Fed. Unemployment Taxes Owed) — 371
- Accrued State Unemployment Taxes (State Unemployment Taxes Owed) — 372
- Accrued Real Estate Taxes (Real Estate Taxes Owed) — 381
- Accrued Federal Income Taxes (Federal Income Taxes Owed) — 391
- Accrued State Income Taxes (State Income Taxes Owed) — 392

Long-Term Obligations (401-450)
- Notes Payable — Long-Term — 401
- Mortgages Payable — 411

OWNERSHIP EQUITY (451-500)

- *Capital Investment (Investment in Business) — 451
- **Capital Stock (Stock Issued) — 461
- *Drawings (Cash Used Personally) — 481
- Retained Earnings (Profit Not Spent) — 491

*For use only by sole owners or partners
**For use only by corporations

Account No.

PROFIT OR LOSS STATEMENT (Accounts 501-999)

Sales and Other Income (501-550)

Sales of Merchandise	501
Sales Returns and Allowances	502
Cash Discounts Allowed (Discounts to Customers)	503
Service Charges	511
Rental Income	521
Cash Discounts Taken (Discounts from Suppliers)	531
Miscellaneous Income	541

Cost of Goods Sold (551-600)

Cost of Merchandise Sold	551
Freight on Purchases	561

Cost of Business Operations (601-700)

Wages	601
Labor from Agencies	602
Supplies	611
Tools	612
Rental of Equipment	621
Repairs to Equipment and Machinery	631
Repairs to Trucks	632
Truck maintenance (Gas and Oil for Trucks)	641

Selling Expenses (701-750)

Advertising	701
Automobile Expenses — Salesmen	711
Commissions	721
Entertainment Expenses	731
Travel Expenses	741

Administrative Expenses (General Expenses) (751-800)

Salaries	751
Office Supplies	761
Postage	762
Telephones	763
Dues & Subscriptions	764
Insurance — Miscellaneous	771
Group Insurance	772
Workmen's Compensation Insurance	773
Automobile Expense	781
Professional Services	786
Bad Debts	791
Interest	796

Account No.

Miscellaneous Expenses (801-850)

Building Expenses (851-900)	
Rent	851
Repairs to Building	861
Utilities	871

Depreciation (901-950)	
Depreciation — Buildings	911
Depreciation — Automobiles	916
Depreciation — Furniture and Office Equipment	921
Depreciation — Machinery	926
Depreciation — Tools	931
Amortization — Rented Property Improvements	946

Taxes (951-999)	
FICA Taxes	951
Unemployment Taxes	952
Real Estate Taxes	961
Miscellaneous Taxes	962
Federal Income Taxes	991
State Income Taxes	992

INCOME AND EXPENSE RECORDS

Any bookkeeping system has two basic parts: a record of income and a record of expenses. There are many different ways of keeping these records, but we will talk about a simple way that saves time and still provides the information you need to make day-to-day and long-term decisions.

Tracking Income A record of income is commonly called the income ledger or sales journal or cash receipts journal. At the very least, you must enter the date, a description of the transaction (such as the check number and customer name), the amount of the transaction, and an indication of the category it goes into from your chart of accounts.

With some creative thinking you could even adapt a simple check ledger, like the one that you get with the checks you order from your bank (*see Figure* 2.2).

Or you can order deposit slips in what is called "two-up" or "side-by-side" format, slip a piece of carbon paper in, and make your record that way (*see Figure* 2.3). If you want to go an extra step and use actual ledger paper, the accompanying illustration shows what your page might look like (*see Figure* 2.4).

Fig. 2.2   Checkbook Ledger

Fig. 2.3   Deposit Slips

DEPOSIT TICKET

NOTICE: A HOLD FOR UNCOLLECTED FUNDS MAY BE PLACED ON FUNDS DEPOSITED BY CHECK OR SIMILAR INSTRUMENTS. THIS COULD DELAY YOUR ABILITY TO WITHDRAW SUCH FUNDS. THE DELAY, IF ANY, WOULD NOT EXCEED THE PERIOD OF TIME PERMITTED BY LAW.

ADDRESS _____

DEPOSIT TICKET

NOTICE: A HOLD FOR UNCOLLECTED FUNDS MAY BE PLACED ON FUNDS DEPOSITED BY CHECK OR SIMILAR INSTRUMENTS. THIS COULD DELAY YOUR ABILITY TO WITHDRAW SUCH FUNDS. THE DELAY, IF ANY, WOULD NOT EXCEED THE PERIOD OF TIME PERMITTED BY LAW.

ADDRESS _____

Left ticket

DATE / DATE _____

	WHO	CHECK# DOLLARS	CENTS
CURRENCY			
COIN			
CHECKS LIST SEPARATELY			
1	4B	119	
2	TenSpeed	19405	
3	Noreh	292	

3/16
3/18
3/20

⑆⑆121000⋮248⑈

CLAUDE F. WHITMYER

TOTAL DEPOSIT

TOTAL

Right ticket

DATE _____

		DOLLARS	CENTS
CURRENCY			
COIN			
CHECKS LIST SEPARATELY			
1	11-24	187	77
2	90-0094	2000	00
3	11-24	120	00

⑆⑆121000⋮248⑈

CLAUDE F. WHITMYER

TOTAL DEPOSIT 2307 77

TOTAL 2307 77

Fig. 2.4　　Income and Expense Ledger

		1		2	3	4	5	6
	CK NO	DATE	CK AMT	DEP AMT		BAL FORWARD 3174.96	ACCOUNT	AMOUNT
1 Sol Columbus	364	2/12	11000			306496	PRINTING	11000
2 US Post Office	365	2/20	9750			296746	POSTAGE	9750
3 Sol Columbus	366	2/24	11000			285746	PRINTING	11000
4 Tom Hargadon	367	2/28	20000			265746	RENT	20000
5								
6 SF SPCA		3/1	60000	60000		325746	CONSULTING	60000
7 Gail Grimes		3/2	3457				BOOK SALES	3457
8 Terry McHugh		3/2	14000	45457			TUITION	14000
9 Gail Grimes		3/2	14000				TUITION	14000
10 Joan Taylor		3/2	14000			371203	TUITION	14000
11 Whole Earth Access	368	3/3	15374			355829	OFC EXP	15374
12								
13							SUMMARY	
14								
15							INCOME	
16							CONSULTING	60000
17							BOOKS	3457
18							TUITION	42000
19								105457
20							EXPENSES	
21							PRINTING	22000
22							POSTAGE	9750
23							RENT	20000
24							OFC EXP	15374
25								61124
26								
27							PROFIT	44333

Tracking Expenses For expenses you need exactly the same information: date, description, amount, and category. Again the simple checkbook ledger from the bank can serve this function (*see Figure* 2.2), or you can have a more elaborate system, such as a cash disbursements journal, which allows you to summarize the most important items by "spreading" them in columns to the left of the basic information (*see Figure* 2.4).

Many people use credit cards to make purchases. This can be convenient, but it can also get out of control if you neglect to post credit card receipts in your expense record. We recommend that you not use credit cards for business purposes. Then they won't be a problem, and you won't have to pay the high interest rates. If you must use credit cards, then keep a record of your purchases just as though you had paid cash. If you record these purchases in the same ledger as your actual cash expenditures, then give them a separate page or column, or otherwise clearly distinguish them as credit card purchases. This is to avoid entering them twice (double posting) when you make the actual payment to the credit card company. Another simple approach is to pay the entire balance due on each monthly statement (thus avoiding interest charges) and allocating the detail of the various purchases to their proper categories. This would be done in the spreadsheet columns of your cash disbursements journal.

Preprinted Ledgers Most office supply stores sell simple bookkeeping systems that you can use by filling in the blanks. The two most common are Ekonomik and Dome. These come in formats that are laid out for specific businesses—beauty parlor, gas station, retail store, real estate, construction, and so on—one of which may be suitable for your business. The main difference between them is that the Dome format is vertical, while Ekonomik's is horizontal. As most people find it easier to read numbers laid out across the page, we prefer the Ekonomik system, but both work. Whichever you choose will make your bookkeeping life much simpler.

One-Write Systems A one-write check writing system can save a lot of time. With the writing of each check, all records that you need are made. It consists of special checks that have a strip of carbon on the back, about one-half inch wide, running the length of the check. You place the check on your check ledger page and fill it out. As you write, a carbon copy is being made in the ledger. At the end of a page or the end of a month, you simply get out the adding machine and total up the columns for a summary of your expenditures for a certain period. It takes a little practice to keep the checks lined up with the right line of the ledger, but before long you will find yourself spending half as much time on check writing. Most of the vendors that sell these systems also offer window envelopes, so, after filling out the name and address lines on your one-write check, you can just slip it in the window and mail it.

Most one-write systems provide areas for deposits and running cash balances. Many businesses use these journals as their entire bookkeeping system.

They give the totals to their tax preparer at the end of the year, thus avoiding the marathon of pain that otherwise awaits them in April.

Systems for keeping track of clients and vendors are also available. If you write more than thirty checks each month, and you are not ready to move up to a computer program, one-write is the system to use.

FINANCIAL STATEMENTS

Summarizing your bookkeeping and inventory records into financial statements will give you important information about the condition of your business. The two most common financial statements are the income statement and the balance sheet. As they are drawn from your written record of the money going into and out of your business, they are not difficult to create. By preparing and reviewing financial statements regularly, you can get the answers to many questions such as: How profitable is this business? What do the business assets look like? What changes have taken place between months or years? Which costs are a problem? How much is owed on debts of various kinds?

For efficient use of your financial statements, put them on the wall, where you can refer to them easily and regularly. This is the best way to gain a real grasp of what is happening in the day-to-day operation of the business. At the same time you will begin to see the weekly, monthly, or yearly patterns unique to your business.

Fig. 2.5   Profit and Loss Statement

LIVING LIGHTLY, INC.
Statement of Profit and Loss
4 Year Summary

	1977	1978	1979	1980
INCOME				
SALES	$2,505	$21,489	$52,730	$289,025
(Returns & Allowances)		(155)	(233)	(8,176)
NET SALES	2,505	21,334	52,497	280,849
COST OF GOODS SOLD	1,927	16,530	40,382	181,625
GROSS PROFIT	578	4,804	12,115	99,224
GROSS MARGIN	23%	23%	23%	35%
EXPENSES				
Advertising & Promotional	147	1,668	2,039	13,974
Auto & Truck	-	-	-	1,319
Bank Charges	11	-	-	1,588
Cash Short/(Over)	-	-	-	2,791
Depreciation & Amort.	44	126	178	1,105
Dues & Publications	8	-	-	213
Health Benefits	-	-	-	370
Insurance	-	-	-	1,120
Office Supplies	192	783	1,248	3,081
Payroll - Taxes	-	-	-	8,000
Payroll - Wages	-	-	-	26,506
Professional - Leg. & Acct.	5	-	-	1,532
Professional - Other	-	-	-	1,588
Rent	250	1,315	3,750	22,100
Repairs & Maintenance	-	204	-	282
Taxes & Licenses	-	583	1,345	614
Telephone	33	-	-	3,073
Travel & Entertainment	-	-	230	1,380
Utilities	-	518	451	1,760
Miscellaneous	-	38	963	879
TOTAL EXPENSES	690	5,235	10,204	93,275
NET PROFIT/(LOSS)	(112)	(431)	1,911	5,988
CUMULATIVE PROFIT/(LOSS)	(112)	(543)	1,368	7,356

The Income Statement

An income statement (sometimes called a profit and loss statement or simply the P&L) shows the sources of income, the costs and expenses of running the business, and the amount of profit or loss left over.

The Balance Sheet

A balance sheet shows what the business owns and what it owes. What you own is reported in various categories, such as cash in bank, accounts receivable, furniture and fixtures, and so forth. These are known as assets. What you owe is reported in categories such as accounts payable, or long-term notes payable. These are known as liabilities. The balance sheet also shows your claim against the business as its owner. This claim is known as owner's equity.

The balance sheet is connected to the income statement by the fact that owner's equity increases and decreases by the amount of profit or loss that the business makes over time.

Other Financial Statements

Two other statements can be useful to small businesses. A statement of changes in financial position shows the origin of all the money flowing into and out of the business, and the use it was put to. It is similar to the income statement except that it goes a step further to include additional capital or loans, that is, money brought into the business that is not income from sales. It also shows all capital expenditures (on furniture or equipment, etc.) as well as owner's draw (the money taken from the business by the owner). A statement of retained earnings shows how much the net income was, and what portion was taken out or distributed, what portion was used by the business and how much is still available for use.

INVENTORY

For a service business with over $500 worth of office supplies, and for any business that sells a product, it makes good sense to keep a written record of supplies and products on hand. If there are few items, you need only count them periodically and write the number down. You will quickly note any discrepancies between what is supposed to be on hand and what you counted. But when you have more than a dozen items, it helps to create a more systematic method of tracking your inventory.

Manufacturer's Inventory

Manufacturers need a different kind of inventory control than retailers or distributors. Many manufacturing businesses are seasonal and have alternating

Fig. 2.6   Balance Sheet

```
                    LIVING LIGHTLY, INC.


                     December 31,1980
                      Balance Sheet

Current Assets:

          Cash On Hand              300.00
          Cash In Banks         (6,450.52)
          Accounts Receivable   24,287.02
          Inventory             65,890.56
          Security Deposits      4,218.00

      Total Current Assets                    $88,245.06

Fixed Assets:
          Furniture & Fixtures   7,597.64
      Total Fixed Assets                        7,597.64

TOTAL ASSETS                                  $95,842.70


Liabilities

          Accounts Payable      52,330.80
          Payroll Taxes          5,716.84
          Sales Tax              7,984.15
          Notes Payable-Officers 4,560.00
          Accrued Salaries       5,150.91
      Total Liabilities                       $75,742.70

Capital

          Common Stock          20,100.00
          Retained Earnings          0.00
          Current Profit/Loss        0.00
      Total Capital                            20,100.00

TOTAL LIABILITIES & CAPITAL                   $95,842.70
```

peak periods of sales demand followed by slow periods. Sales trends must be carefully monitored so that there is just enough inventory on hand to meet the minimum production cycle requirements. This is tricky, which is why it's important to build inventory systems into the business at the start.

Let's say that you sell a mustache grooming kit, made up of mustache wax, a mustache comb, a high-quality pair of trimming scissors, and the packaging materials. You know that you can sell five thousand units for Christmas. With a good inventory tracking system, you would know from previous years that most of the orders for the Christmas retail season are received by July. You would also know that you need to order the primary ingredients, beeswax and fragrance, sixty days before you want to begin assembling the order. The bottles and caps need forty-five days, and the comb and scissors might require thirty days of lead time. The labels also take thirty days. You need two weeks to put together the five thousand kits. So you must order wax and fragrance for delivery in early August; bottles and caps for mid-August; comb, scissors, and labels for early September; and so on. Notice that you have allowed yourself less than two weeks of grace if anything goes wrong.

Clearly, this is a complicated set of variables. To add to the complication, you have only two other peaks, neither as big as Christmas, but each big enough to merit attention: Valentine's Day and Father's Day. You have to repeat the same evaluation and staggered ordering process for those two holidays. You know how many kits you might sell this year, from the sales records you kept last year and previous years. You know the quantity of beeswax, fragrance, bottles, and labels you have on hand from the inventory tally sheets you completed last week. You know lead times on additional ingredients and packaging from your accounts payable records. You know how long it takes to assemble the kits from the work record you keep, or from the invoices of the subcontractors you hired to do the assembly last time. With all of these pieces you can foresee your needs and make management decisions based on what has worked in the past.

Retail and Distributor Inventory

Retailers and distributors on the other hand can make purchasing decisions based on a much simpler set of records. They carry many more items for sale and often see small changes in the inventory count on any given item. The most common method is to count the inventory every three months and to keep a paper record of subtractions from and additions to inventory during the intervening months. Every time the inventory is counted, the actual number can be compared with the paper number to see what has been lost or broken, which is called "shrinkage." Beyond this record, rates of sale on an item-by-item basis can be made.

Fig. 2.7 Inventory Worksheet

INVENTORY WORK SHEET

DEPARTMENT: (1)
VENDOR: (2)
TAKEN BY: DATE: (3)
CALCULATED BY: (4)

ITEM (5)	OUR COST (6)	BEGINNING INVENTORY (7)	GOODS RECEIVED (8)	ENDING INVENTORY (9)	EXTENSION (10)	RATE OF SALE (11)

To use this worksheet make as many copies as you need and fill in the blanks as follows:

(1) This is used if you want to track different sources of income, or to make ordering easier. A grocery store might have a dairy department, dry goods, meat, liquor, and so forth. A woodstove distributor might have stoves, stovepipe, and fireplace accessories.

(2) For ordering purposes you would keep a separate inventory sheet for each vendor. Use this to tell them apart.

(3) Inventory is such a big job, that often you will get help to make the job easier. Whoever does the actual physical counting of the items listed on each sheet, should sign here. This person should also fill in the date that the count is made on here.

(4) Whoever uses the adding machine to make the below calculations should sign here.

(5) This is to describe the item. You can use the vendors ordering codes, or make up descriptions that make sense to you.

(6) This is the unit price that your supplier charges you for the item.

(7) This is how many units of the item were in inventory when you completed last month's count. So each beginning inventory is always equal to each previous month's ending inventory.

(8) This is how many units you received of each item during the intervening month.

(9) This is the number of units of each item that are physically counted on this date.

(10) This is the product of multiplying (9) by (6), giving you the value of the inventory on hand at the time of this counting.

(11) This is how many units you sold during the last month. You add (7) and (8) and subtract (9) from that sum. Rate of sale equals beginning inventory plus good received during the month, minus ending inventory.

DO YOU NEED A TAX ACCOUNTANT?

Ted Rabinowitsh of Rabinowitsh and Stuart, property managers, prepares his own taxes. "I use a Macintosh program. When they're finished, I go to a really top-flight accountant. I ask him questions I have, and he makes suggestions. Maybe I'm not doing something quite right or not looking at something. Sometimes he helps me with details—sometimes with whole strategies for doing things."

We think Ted's approach is a sound one. In the past, most people with basic arithmetic and the willingness to persevere could figure out their taxes, set up their books, and even incorporate themselves. In fact, doing your own books and taxes was, and is, the surest way of understanding how your business really works. With the passage of the Tax Reform Act of 1986, however, things have changed. We still recommend that you do your own bookkeeping (although, when the volume gets big, you may want to have a competent bookkeeper come in as a subcontractor and do your regular posting). But we have had to re-examine the feasibility of doing your own tax returns.

As the Tax Reform Act has gone into effect, we have noticed—and our accountant and CPA friends have confirmed—that the new tax laws make tax preparation so difficult that it may be smarter to hire a professional than to attempt doing your returns yourself. Admittedly, tax professionals have a vested interest in a recommendation like this. Even in the past, however, we have seen the advice of professionals pay off in tax savings over time, for instance, for people who had several ventures that greatly complicated their tax situation, or for people who had too little time to stay current on tax laws. So, after careful consideration, we think the wisest course today is to hire a tax professional. At the same time, you should know all the records a tax preparer needs so that you can have completed most of the work yourself, thus keeping your costs to a minimum.

RESOURCES

Mary Lee Dyer, *Practical Bookkeeping for the Small Business* (Chicago: Contemporary Books, Inc., 1976). A good workbook to help you keep your double entry bookkeeping straight.

Bernard Kamaroff, *Small-Time Operator* (Laytonville, California: Bell Springs Press, 1987). The best book for single entry bookkeeping.

Tax Guide for Small Businesses, IRS Publication No. 334 (revised yearly). Covers every aspect of small business taxes. Available from any IRS office.

There are many companies that sell one-write systems (called peg board systems too). Here are the names of a few:

Ekonomik Systems
P.O. Box 11413
Tacoma, WA 98411
206-475-0292

New England Business Systems
500 North Main Street
Groton, MA 01471
1-800-225-6380

McBee Systems
151 Corlandt Street
Belleville, NJ 07109
201-759-6500

Safeguard Business Systems, Inc.
455 Maryland Avenue
Fort Washington, PA 19034
215-641-5000

Standard Accounting Systems
P.O. Box 20609
Portland, OR 97220
1-800-547-9972

3

Financial Strategies

After you have bookkeeping systems in place, you can start thinking about the financial management side of your business. This is different from the physical fact of tracking your day-to-day finances through bookkeeping. It concerns the larger picture—multiple sources of income, pricing, billing, cash flow, budgeting, meeting the ongoing need for working capital. How well your business does will be largely determined by your skill in managing these basic business principles.

SOURCES OF INCOME

Two main rules regarding sources of income can make or break your one-person business: First, focus on doing just one business. Second, within that focus, create a variety of income streams.

Focus on Doing Just One Business

The rule about doing just one business seems obvious but is ignored. It seems obvious because it is difficult enough to master a single business. It is ignored, especially by newer businesses, because of the tendency to try to do anything for anybody as long as you're paid for it, and whether or not it's appropriate to the business you're trying to define. Start-up businesses often have to spend considerable time defining their product or service in a focused way that is easy for others to understand. Yet this is the way to continue to receive a stable flow of referrals as the business grows and matures.

Almost any business field has a highly specialized language and a body of traditional knowledge, both of which are gained from experience. Some fields are mastered only after years. Because knowledge based on experience is so important to success, it is a powerful strategy to focus on one field and get good at it. Still, there is a fine line to walk in deciding when different sources of income are related enough to be considered part of the same business. Our goal in the following discussion is to help you learn when you need to gather your income sources together more, and when you can branch out.

Create a Variety of Income Streams

When we talk about creating a variety of income streams, we mean, first, having more than one client and, second, having diverse sources of income.

In the first case, it is dangerous if more than fifty percent of your income comes from one client. For many new businesses, this may be the company you left to start your own firm. It doesn't take a vivid imagination to see what the effects of losing that client might be.

Valerie Skonie left a sales management job to start a service that provides technically specialized sales people to firms like the one she left. Her former employer became her first, and biggest, client. She knew she needed more clients because the person who had chosen her firm might leave, and the successor might drop her. Or internal policy could change, canceling the service or bringing it in-house, so that outside sales people would no longer be needed. Clearly, Valerie's immediate priority was to find other clients.

Less obvious was the case of Arlen, a graphic designer and writer, who did five different newsletters for a large bank for six years. Because he worked for five different department heads, he had a sense of security based on the diversity of income sources within the company. During a financial crisis, however, the bank management introduced a policy against outside contractors, and Arlen had to start his business all over again.

The need for having different sources of income is harder to explain. The purpose of this kind of variety is twofold:

- To provide the one-person business with good market information and long-term training
- To offer protection against naturally occurring fluctuations in income, to which one-person businesses are especially vulnerable

At the same time, all the sources of income need to be related within the definition of what the business is.

Photographer Norman Prince gets income from selling direct services as a photographer, teaching classes in photography, and selling stock photos (stock photos are originals, usually used in textbooks, of "stock" subjects like Mt. Rainier, the Lincoln Memorial, or a Flamenco guitarist). All of these sources of income are from the same field. Besides bringing fun and variety into Norman's life, this approach gives him information on several markets in his field, and it helps him develop new skills. He learns about changing market forces by, for instance, noticing that more stock requests are coming from England, many of them specifying pets and other animals. This alerts him to a possible future market for his services as an assignment photographer. Or he may find more students in his classes asking about how to photograph pets, alerting him to a new market before most other photographers notice it. Most important, having to keep current in multiple aspects of his field is a form of training that will keep Norman a technically skilled person as long as he is active in business.

Debra Dadd has a variety of income sources, too. She is a pioneer in the field of education about "in-home and personal environmental toxins." Debra writes books, publishes a newsletter, gives speeches, and does consulting, both in person and by telephone—all on this one subject. From these various income sources she gains information about new markets. In addition, each part of the business feeds the other parts. Writing books generates publicity tours with radio and TV guest appearances, which in turn sells more books, newsletters, and consulting. On tour she learns about interests in different parts of the country and hears about emerging areas of controversy in which she needs to develop expertise. Her private clients bring up questions, concerns, and experiences that she can use in her newsletter, which in turn provides material for additional books. Debra's is a superb example of how useful variety in income sources can be, since it contributes to the business in so many ways.

How to Protect Against Income Fluctuations

The best protection against the ups and downs of income is a broad client base that will provide the variety of income sources you need in order to keep your income on as even a path as possible. To build this base you need to select your customers purposefully, with specific objectives in mind. You must also track your income sources in some detail and frequently review your pricing, your policies, and all other practices you use to attract customers.

In setting objectives for the selection of customers or clients, keep in mind three key problems of one-person businesses: (1) income streams tend to be volatile, (2) there is a constant need to upgrade your skills, and (3) the nature of your business is constantly changing. As your client base broadens, you should continually monitor it to see if you are attracting the variety of customers necessary to respond to these problems. Build these sources of income into your financial statements by tracking them in your income records. This will amount to a regular audit of your progress in selecting customers with an organized intent.

Clients To Help Combat Income Volatility. To deal with income volatility, you might focus on three types of clients: Repeat clients, appreciative clients, and flexible clients.

Repeat clients are desirable because they don't have to be resold on what you do, and they understand how your work or product meets their needs. Some repeat customers may not need you often, or even for many years (if you are an orthodontist, for example). Some repeat business is unpredictable (as with morticians and obstetricians). Still, repeat clients are at the core of most businesses (except tourist businesses and once in a lifetime expenditures such as a trip to Antarctica).

In your search for repeat clients you might emphasize customers who are likely to use you frequently, as well as those who will need you at seasonally slack times. For example, a gardener would find desirable a client who would need weekly maintenance all year as well as tree pruning in the winter.

Appreciative clients are those who feel that you do an especially good job and that find your work is just right for them. They therefore refer other clients to you. The more appreciative clients you have, the fewer unappreciative clients you'll have to take. Unappreciative clients are more likely to create conflict, complain about you to others, dawdle on their payments, and require you to repair problems that you didn't cause. You can develop appreciative clients by noting how your work or product might be most beneficial to them. In professional sales parlance this is called "selling the benefits."

Flexible clients are almost a must for many one-person businesses. Small businesses typically find themselves either swamped with jobs and customers or doing and selling nothing. Therefore, a client who will agree to adjust the work schedule or delivery time, to accept work on a smaller scale or shipment of a portion of an order, or to postpone the transaction until another mutually beneficial time, is immensely valuable. In many businesses you can find clients who are willing to be flexible.

Clients to Help You Upgrade Your Skills In a one-person business it is essential to keep your skills sharpened and up-to-date so that you remain at the top of your field. Two types of clients will make a big difference in this regard: challenging clients and clients that will give you a chance to learn on the job.

When you take on a client who challenges you to use your best skills and most imaginative approach, the work becomes rewarding in itself. You are also encouraged to refine those skills that are not called for in every job or product sale.

Clients who offer a chance to learn are also extremely desirable because they help you grow. Such clients will want you to do something you haven't done, or will let you try something entirely new. Each such opportunity gives you a chance to talk to your peers, and to ask questions that will keep you in touch with the mainstream of your field.

A chimney sweep who decides to replace some ornamental tiles for the first time might need to meet tile setters and learn about the new uses of tiles in fireplaces. And learning from the tile setter might also bring the chance to be recommended to new clients.

Nearly all businesses are in flux. In fields that change rapidly (medicine, dentistry, nursing, tax law) in-service training is required to maintain a license. In most other fields too, the knowledge base is changing, and you need ways to expand yourself. The client who gives you a chance to learn is your form of continuing education.

Clients to Help You Respond to Business Changes Because business is always changing, you need a way to keep in touch with the direction in which your field is moving. So consider two other criteria for establishing your client base: Make it as broad as possible, and as diverse as possible.

Having a broad base of clients means that you try to serve a wide variety of clients by offering a range of services that will extend your business into interesting and possibly expanding fields. Having a diverse base means catering to customers with an unusually wide range of needs. For example, a restaurant with a broad customer base might attract teenagers and old people, local folks and travelers. If it had a diverse base as well, it would serve vegetarians, alcohol drinkers, nonsmokers, and hot Texas chili fans.

These examples are intended to be humorous and to make a point. Serving teenagers would have alerted you to the pizza trend early, serving older people to the low cholesterol trend, serving vegetarians and nonsmokers to the astounding increase in their numbers. And that's the point: A broad and diverse base will alert you to trends.

The problem when you have a broad and diverse clientele is to stay focused on running just one business. Here are some examples of people we know who have succeeded:

A management consultant to large companies who takes on a few smaller clients and a few nonprofit organizations, teaches classes at a local college, and has several international clients.

An astrologer with regular office clients who sees a few low-income clients at a local psychic research center, writes magazine columns, and markets a selection of his ten favorite occult books wherever he goes.

A graphic artist who does a newsletter for one large corporate client, has several dozen small clients, draws her own cartoon strip for a neighborhood newspaper, occasionally designs sets and images for a local TV station, has a low-priced special service for restaurant menus, and is a prominent partner in a local photography gallery.

PRICING FOR YOUR PRODUCT OR SERVICES

Some businesses don't have to worry about pricing because there is already a market price for their goods or services. An example is the price for developing a role of 35-mm color film at a Fotomat franchise shop. But most businesses have to decide how to price their goods or service and whether it will be below, equal to, or above the market price.

The price you can charge above that needed to cover overhead is usually not a matter of supply and demand, although traditional economists would tell you otherwise. For most businesses, the price charged determines the type of client the business will have, not the number. A low price may attract few customers and a high price can bring in many.

The price of a good or service tells the customer what they can expect from the business. A low price often means little service, mostly self-help, and a poor refund policy; with a service business it implies amateurism and inexperience. A high price means the opposite. Prices that are out of line with those of similar businesses need to be justified to customers through added value. Customers will sort themselves out according to the value they want, and those who choose your business will do so because you meet or exceed their expectations.

For example, a marketing research consultant who charges $1,000 per focus group research session will be expected to show up twenty minutes before the session to discuss it with the the client. Afterward the consultant will deliver an audiotape and a one-page summary of the session. The same consultant charging $2,000 per session will be expected to meet with the client for at least an hour during the week before the session, to hold the session in an interview room with a two-way mirror and video camera, and to deliver a five- to ten-page summary a few weeks later, together with a verbal presentation. The pricing determines the client's expectations.

As publisher Bear Kamaroff explains, "Pricing is subjective. You have to charge enough to make it a job worth doing—so that it pays for itself. And you can't charge so much that people are put off by the price.

"I based my pricing of *Small-Time Operator* on what the book cost me to make and on the level of discount I have to give to the people I usually sell to. I also experimented a little. If the book sells for $10 and I have to give a sixty percent discount to my wholesaler, I receive $4. Printing costs $1.50 a book. So I have $2.50 left to cover my incidental expenses and overhead. Does this price earn me enough to make me happy? If it is worth doing, is $10 a fair price for the book? Will people pay that price?

"I did market research at bookstores to see what other books were selling for, and I talked to people in and out of the book trade. I didn't want anybody to turn the book down because of the price. And I didn't want anybody to buy it in spite of the price.

"Pricing is not that important to a lot of people, particularly with small businesses. People are more interested in quality than price. If you're a good auto mechanic, customers will happily pay you $35 an hour rather than risk leaving their car with someone they don't know who charges $20 an hour. Unless it gets outrageous, price will not scare people away."

Pricing Guidelines for Product Businesses

If you are a manufacturer, distributor, or retailer of products, you need to consider several factors in setting the price for your product.

1. Return on investment pricing Sometimes you simply base your price on the amount of profit you want to make. This is especially likely if you are a manufacturer or distributor, and you expect to sell several thousand of a particular product in a given period of time. Suppose you are a fireplace accessory distributor. You have kept good books so you know what your fixed expenses usually are, and you can estimate with some confidence your variable expenses. In a typical winter season, from September through January, your fixed expenses run $1,000 per month and your variable expenses total around $6,000. You expect to sell 3,000 fireplace tool sets during the five-month period. The sets cost you $11 each, or $33,000 for the lot. You would like to earn at least a ten percent profit. To find out how much you must charge, add $5,000 fixed expenses, $6,000 variable expenses, and $33,000 cost of goods sold, which totals $44,000. Multiply $44,000 by 1.1 to get the total with a ten percent profit: $48,400. Now divide by 3,000, the number of tool sets. You get $16.13, the price you must charge per set if you want to cover all costs and make a ten percent profit. But there are many other factors that might affect the price.

2. Fair Trade Laws Many states have fair trade laws that allow the manufacturer of a product to make agreements with retailers and distributors about how to price the product. If you live in one of these states, you may have to price your products with that in mind.

3. Manufacturers' suggested prices This is a little different from fair trade laws. The manufacturer tries to protect the quality image of the product or the profit margins of their retailers, without the aid of fair trade laws. So you may have to price your product according to a schedule suggested by the manufacturer.

4. Nationally advertised prices As a retailer or distributor you can often get away with undercutting the prices that manufacturers advertise in national media. However, it is very difficult to charge more than that, regardless of how well you can justify it from an expense point of view.

5. Pricing policies of others in the field If other businesses carry products of similar quality or type, you must be aware of their prices and be prepared to explain to your customers why you charge a different price, whether it is higher or lower.

6. Market strategy If you clearly tell your customers what makes your products different, and that difference includes price, you can sometimes create a market niche by the price you charge. You may choose to do this as a part of an overall market strategy. The simplest example is of a business that sets prices and offers quality in a range not served by others in the field.

7. Type of merchandise The type of products you sell can also influence pricing. Convenience stores, such as neighborhood grocers, or national chains like 7-11, can charge more for the items you might otherwise buy in a supermarket, simply because they are open late at night or are located nearby. Special interest stores generally charge more for an item than a department store. Many of the services or products that a one-person business might offer could easily be priced by the convenience or special interest value that they offer.

8. Seasonal nature of sales If you typically have good and bad times during the year, you might set your prices higher during the up times and lower during the down in order to stimulate sales.

9. Desired customers All other factors being accounted for, you will attract more affluent customers if you charge a higher price. A lower price will attract more price-conscious shoppers.

How to Price a New Product

Few people ever have the need to price a new product, but if you do, remember two things: First, customers will evaluate the reasonableness of your price by finding something to compare your product to. Sony's Walkman, which was a completely new concept, was priced at $300 when it was introduced in Japan, because it was compared by customers to similar portable objects such as cameras, portable radio headsets, and walkie-talkies, which were also in the $300 price range at that time. It was first sold in fancy camera shops, with a case like that for a camera. In setting your price, therefore, try to figure out the products that will be compared with yours, and take those prices into account.

Second, the wholesale price of products is usually half the retail price. So if you can discover how much knowledgeable buyers of your product would pay at wholesale, you can double this to get your retail price. Often products and services that are new to consumers have been known by professionals in the field for some time. Such was the case with automatic coffee brewing machines and automobile buying services.

How to Price Professional Services

In pricing a service business you should ask three basic questions:
- How much money do I want to take home?
- How many hours do I want to work?
- How much money do I want above my living and business expenses?

The money you take home will determine the lifestyle you can afford. The number of hours you work will help determine your schedule. The money you want above your expenses will be that amount you can put away for vacations, old age, spontaneous adventures, and so forth.

Calculating how much to charge isn't difficult, but first you must understand the difference between productive and administrative time, also called billable and nonbillable time. Understanding this difference is crucial to deciding how much you want to work. Work includes all the hours you pay bills, do bookkeeping, and tend to filing and marketing activities, as well as the things you do that you can charge a fee for, or the time you spend selling a product. First figure out how many hours of administrative time you must spend for each hour of productive time. Then use the accompanying exercise to calculate your rate. Another way you might price your service is to ask others in your field how they do it.

Photographer Norman Prince uses a combination of pricing strategies. "I go mostly by the American Society of Magazine Photographers average prices. My stock clients, most of whom are book publishers, pay those prices these days. When I'm working on assignment, I look at the ASMP price ranges for assignment work, which are just average prices being paid in the country as of a certain date for this type of work. I try to position myself somewhere in that range. When I'm doing editorial work I charge a day rate, which is fairly standard. But when I did industrial work recently I was able to get much more than I normally would. Whatever the job I always listen to what people have to say about their budgets. And when I'm working for nonprofits, especially ones run by friends, I try to give them a fair, reasonable price."

Setting Fees for Professional Services

This exercise will help you figure out the minimum fee to charge your clients. The calculations are based on how much income you want to earn, how many days you wish to work, your anticipated expenses, and how much profit you would like to set aside in addition to salary and business expenses.

Each line of the worksheet is numbered to correspond to the instructions below. Following these instructions will make it easier to complete the form. The blank form explains all the entries and calculations you should make. We have also included an example that is filled in.

The first step is to fill in the blanks for
    Yearly Salary (1),
    Days worked per month (2a),
    Days worked per year (2b), and
    Desired Percent Profit (3).

There is no magic formula for answering these questions. They are simply personal choices that you must make. How much money do you need to spend on your personal lifestyle? How hard and how often do you want to work? How much of each dollar you bring in would you like to set aside for the future?

The second step is to calculate your EXPENSES (4).

The blanks on the form may or may not represent some or all of your expense items. They are provided to stimulate your thinking. Be sure to include any additional items that may apply to your business.

The third step is to add up the columns to get TOTAL EXPENSES (5).

The final step is to make a few calculations and fill in the
    Daily Overhead (6),
    Daily Salary (7),
    Revenue Requirement (8), and
    Daily Profit (9).

Now fill in the "Required Billing Rate" (10) by adding up (6) through (9). This is your "day rate," or what you should try to make per day.

If you want to know your "Equivalent Hourly Rate" (11), divide the "Required Billing Rate" (10) by the number of billable hours worked per day. (In the example it is six hours.)

Fig. 3.1   Worksheet for Calculating Fees

<u>**Worksheet for Calculating Fees**</u>

1 - Yearly Salary   ———— *(Supply the salary you wish to earn.)*
2a - Days worked per month ———— *(Supply the number of days per month you wish to work.)*
2b - Days worked per year ———— Multiply 12 months by number of days you wish to work per month.
3 - Desired Percent Profit ———— *(Supply the percent profit you want.)*

4 - EXPENSES *(Fill in the lines below for your expenses.)*

	Monthly		Yearly
Operation Overhead			
Office Expenses			
Rent	————	x 12 =	————
Office help	————	x 12 =	————
Postage	————	x 12 =	————
Telephone	————	x 12 =	————
Utilities	————	x 12 =	————
Other	————	x 12 =	————
Subtotal			
Support Services			
Insurance	————	x 12 =	————
Marketing	————	x 12 =	————
Legal & Accounting	————	x 12 =	————
Promotion	————	x 12 =	————
Other	————	x 12 =	————
Subtotal			
Additional Expenses			
Automobile	————	x 12 =	————
Entertainment	————	x 12 =	————
Travel	————	x 12 =	————
Vacation	————	x 12 =	————
Miscellaneous	————	x 12 =	————
Subtotal			

5 - TOTAL EXPENSES *(Add the expense figures and put total here.)* = ————

6 - Daily Overhead ———— *(Divide total yearly expenses by number of days worked per year.)*
7 - Daily Salary ———— *(Divide total yearly salary by number of days worked per year.)*
8 - Revenue Requirement ———— *(Sum of Daily Overhead (6) and Daily 'Salary' (7).)*
9 - Daily Profit ———— *(Multiply Desired Percent Profit (3) by Revenue Requirement (8) and divide by 100.)*

10 - Required Billing Rate ———— *(Add Daily Overhead (6), Daily Salary (7), and Daily Profit (8).)*
11 - Equivalent Hourly Rate ———— *(Divide Required Billing Rate by the number of billable hours worked per day.)*

Fig. 3.1   Worksheet for Calculating Fees

<u>**Example**</u>

1 - Yearly Salary	$48,000.00
2a - Days worked per month	20
2b - Days worked per year	240
3 - Desired Percent Profit	15

4 - EXPENSES

	Monthly	Yearly
Operation Overhead		
Office Expenses		
Rent	$200.00	$2,400.00
Office help	$200.00	$2,400.00
Postage	$100.00	$1,200.00
Telephone	$200.00	$2,400.00
Utilities	$50.00	$600.00
Other	$200.00	$2,400.00
Subtotal	$950.00	$11,400.00
Support Services		
Insurance	$50.00	$600.00
Marketing	$150.00	$1,800.00
Legal & Accounting	$10.00	$120.00
Promotion	$50.00	$600.00
Other	$40.00	$480.00
Subtotal	$350.00	$4,200.00
Additional Expenses		
Automobile	$125.00	$1,500.00
Entertainment	$200.00	$2,400.00
Travel	$50.00	$600.00
Vacation	$200.00	$2,400.00
Miscellaneous	$100.00	$1,200.00
Subtotal	$675.00	$8,100.00
5 - TOTAL EXPENSES	$1,975.00	$23,700.00

6 - Daily Overhead	$98.75
7 - Daily Salary	$200.00
8 - Revenue Requirements	$298.75
9 - Daily Profit	$44.81

10 - Required Billing Rate	$343.56
11 - Equivalent Hourly Rate	$68.71

How to Do Estimates or Quotes

From time to time you will be asked to submit an estimate or quotation of how much it will cost to complete a project. Should you charge by the hour or the day? Or can you make a close enough guess as to the true costs of completing the project that you can give your potential client a fixed price estimate?

Corporate clients are used to paying by the day or half day, but small businesses often prefer paying by the hour. Many clients prefer to contract for services on a fixed price basis. For you, the major advantage of a fixed price contract is that it gives you the opportunity to make an extra profit by working hard to do better than you estimated. For the client the major benefit is the assurance that you will not go over budget, even if you overrun your estimates.

Making a fixed price contract work depends on your accuracy in estimating direct labor costs and direct expenses. To these you add a figure for overhead (the cost to keep your office open) and the profit you would like to make.

Overhead is usually calculated as a percentage of direct labor. To figure out your overhead rate, add up the total amount you must spend each year to keep your office open, and divide it by the number of days you expect to be billing

Fig. 3.2   Estimating a Fixed Price Contract

Direct Labor

Systems Analyst *(this might be you)*	20 days X $350 =	$ 7,000
Programmer/Analyst *(subcontractor)*	60 days X $275 =	16,500
Clerical/Data Entry *(subcontractor)*	15 days X $100 =	1,500
	TOTAL DIRECT LABOR =	$25,000

Overhead (50% of direct labor) *(from the example)*   = $12,500

Direct Expense

Air fare	$ 1,500
Rental car	500
Meals	500
Hotel	1,000
Modem connect charges	300
Printing *(documentation)*	400
Postage *(express deliveries)*	75
TOTAL DIRECT EXPENSE =	$ 4,275

DIRECT LABOR + OVERHEAD + DIRECT EXPENSE	$41,775
PROFIT *(15% OF $41,775)*	$ 6,266
TOTAL FIXED PRICE	$48,041

clients. The result will be your daily overhead expense. Overhead expenses include rent, utilities, phone, and so forth, as illustrated in the worksheet for calculating fees example on page 47–48. Once you know this figure, you can calculate the average percentage for overhead by dividing yearly overhead by yearly income. On page 49 is a sample worksheet showing how to estimate a fixed price contract for a hypothetical computer programming project (and it would look a lot like this for any service business). We have used the overhead percentage and the percent profit from the previous calculating fees example.

Note that we include the subcontractor fees as part of direct labor when we make the overhead calculation. We are assuming that the subcontractors will require office and administrative help that we must pay for. It is only reasonable to pass this cost on to the client. Because there were no subcontractors included in the calculating fees example, we are assuming the same overhead proportion will be required to support them as to support the primary contractor. With an actual track record, we could be more precise.

Bill Dale, a computer and training consultant, thinks that the biggest problem in pricing service work is failing to estimate accurately the work effort required for a given project. "As a consultant I have only one resource, my time. If I have to put more time into a project, I have lost a part of my fee income." Bill breaks projects down into small steps that are easier to cost out. The typical steps he might use for estimating a training project are:

- Information gathering
- Research
- Development of outline
- Client review(s)
- Revision of outline
- Client review(s)
- Development of material
- Client review(s)
- Revision of material
- Proofing of production
- Proofing of reproduction
- Presentation of materials in training session
- Follow-up immediately after the session: debriefing and summary of course evaluations
- Follow-up in the medium term: effectiveness of training, future needs

As Bill explains further, "I add a fifteen percent contingency to development and then stick to the figure, provided there are no major changes. This is good for the client because he knows what his expenditure will be, and good for me because if I can work quicker or smarter, I will make more money. I don't agree to on-the-spot quotes. I think them through first. In my experience, quoting on the spot always leads to underquoting because I forget a few steps."

How to Do Proposals

There are three common types of proposal that you can offer your clients. First is the "handshake" agreement—a simple verbal agreement that comes from a discussion of what needs to be done, how long it will take, and how much will be charged, including what expenses will be covered. This is the most common form of proposal, and the most risky. Handshake agreements feel good, but it is easy to forget to include key items such as due dates and budget limits. Even if you cover all the bases, no one is infallible. People forget details as time passes, and disagreements about terms can easily arise later. If a client insists on a verbal agreement, your best bet is to take good notes and follow up with a letter that outlines what you think was agreed to. This will give the client a chance to clarify his or her understanding, and in many states such a letter is considered to be a form of contract that can be used later to collect a past-due bill. Without a written agreement it is much harder to collect from a disgruntled client.

The second type of proposal, most often used when dealing with the government or big corporations, is the "fill-out-the-form" proposal. This usually consists of a set of forms supplied by the client, which are very detailed as to the specifications of the project. You are required to complete the forms and submit them along with any supplementary materials you feel are necessary.

The third type of proposal, and the one most often turned to when a written proposal is used, is the letter of agreement. You write a letter to the client that addresses at least these three points: (1) When will the project begin, what will the deadlines for each step of the project be, and when will it be completed? (2) What work will be done, and what will the expenses be? (3) What will the total charge to the client be? A letter of agreement differs from the follow-up letter to the verbal proposal only in its degree of formality. A letter of agreement usually has a signature blank at the end for the client and the contractor to each sign. Copies are retained by each, and the letter is almost sure to be considered a formal contract under the law in most states.

Fig. 3.3   Letter of Agreement

(Date)

(Client Name)
(Client Organization)
(Address)
(City),
(ST) (Zip)

Dear *(Client Name)*:

This letter is to summarize our discussion of *(Date)* and to outline my recommendations for how to proceed in evaluating your approaching need to upgrade the MacDonald Douglas computer systems used by the Shelter, Membership and Accounting departments of the *(Client Organization)*.

Your major concerns seem to lie in three separate areas: 1) When would the best time to upgrade be? 2) What should the future configuration look like and how much would it cost? 3) Will it provide a solution to the problems of processing speed, number of terminals, and present conflicts of use experienced by the Shelter, Membership and Accounting?

I propose to interview the parties affected, do some secondary research on the hardware and software alternatives, and make a recommendation on how to proceed based on my findings.

As always, we will give priority to cultivating practical use of existing computer resources before asking for additional hardware or software.

The outcome of this project will be an update to my previous detailed inventory of the computer hardware and software being used by the Shelter, Membership and Accounting, a clear description of the proposed upgrades, and a recommendation as to how and when to do the proposed switchover to a new system.

I will call you to discuss the steps outlined in this letter. If you approve, I can begin this project the week of *(Date)*. It will take approximately two weeks to complete at a cost of $2,200.00. Expenses such as mileage, phone, photocopies and postage will be billed separately. Payment will be made one-half upon commencement of the work, and one-half upon completion. Additional consulting time will be billed at $60.00 per hour.

If you have any questions, please call me at your earliest convenience.

Sincerely,

(Your Name)

Although proposals are most often thought of in relation to consulting or other service work, they are also a useful tool in the product arena. In this case, you are submitting the proposal to a potential buyer of your goods. A proposal to sell goods should contain clauses describing the type of product, quantity, unit prices, delivery schedules, terms of payment, and any other relevant terms and conditions.

Whether you are in a product or a service business, the use of a written proposal can save you a lot of worry and time by making your agreements clear from the beginning. After a proposal has been accepted, you should follow up with a contract of some sort. In most cases, the proposal itself can serve as the contract.

BILLING AND TERMS

Billing and terms are concerns only if you are offering credit to your clients or customers. Whether you offer credit is often a function of trade practices for your field or product. Manufacturers and distributors almost always have credit programs, and some kinds of retailers offer charge accounts as well. Service businesses, too, frequently offer billing arrangements so that clients pay for the service after it is delivered.

The two questions asked most often are: When should I bill? and What kinds of terms should I offer? The terms of billing arrangements vary by trade or type of product. Terms are specified in that little box on the invoice that says something like "2% 10, Net 30" or "COD" or, as in the letter of agreement above, "Payment will be made one-half upon commencement of the work, and one-half upon completion." Terms are a function of trade practice and cash flow needs. Whenever you offer credit, it costs you something. You may have to borrow working capital to keep going while you wait for payments to come in.

A flat-weave tapestry manufacturing enterprise, Loom Designs, was made up of two one-person businesses. Robert lived in Mexico and handled the supervision of native weavers. Alice lived in San Francisco, California, and handled marketing and selling. When they got a $30,000 order from a large department store, Alice and Robert thought it was wonderful. The terms were net 60 days, and they had enough capital between them to carry their businesses for at least ninety days. Little did they know that the department store was in the habit of paying slowly, and the check didn't arrive for over one hundred days. Because they couldn't be sure when the store would pay, they were each forced to borrow to keep going beyond the ninety days. Naturally they had to pay interest on the borrowed money, even though they used it for only ten days.

Had they known that the large department store habitually paid late, they could have increased the price of the product to compensate for the cost of borrowing the money. Or they might have negotiated a shorter term, maybe net 45 days, so that there was a better chance of getting paid within sixty days.

EXPENSE CONTROL

When you start a business it is hard to estimate how much income you may generate and easy to estimate what your expenses will be. Imagine, for example, setting up a bill-paying service for busy individuals. You might guess that people would pay $15 a month for this service, based on comparable services they buy on a monthly basis. You could estimate the number of people who might sign up if you started by offering the service through CPA friends. There might be two hundred customers the first year, generating about $9,000 total income. So far the key words are *guess, estimate,* and *might.* When it comes to cost, however, you could rehearse the actual operation while paying your own bills. First, you would calculate the time it would take to open the incoming letters, summarize the information on the bills, transfer the figures to a twice-monthly checklist form, mail the form to the customer for approval, and pay the bills in the form and amount the customer might want. You would add to this a rough guess of supply costs and an estimate of the percentage of overhead that could be charged against the business. If you really started the business, you might find that the income was erratic and unpredictable. Even the pricing might need to be changed to match the demand. But your costs would be tangible, hard facts of life that you could find out ahead of time.

The Two-Thirds Rule for Reducing Costs

According to the rule of two-thirds, the best strategy is always to put two-thirds of your energy into reducing costs and one-third into increasing income. The reasoning is that if you do what you can be sure of, you will get a real return on your investment of time and effort.

Your success at generating income is an unknown in the present. You see the results of your effort as you go along. Because creating income can't be hurried up or known for sure in advance, the potential for loss and disappointment is very great. On the other hand, you can decide not to spend, or to reduce spending, in the present. And when you do, you see the results immediately.

Insofar as spending time on something can be wasted, you can lose one-hundred percent of your investment in attempting to generate income, since it might not work. Don't risk your whole business. Put the risk into only one-third of your time and effort.

Even after a business has been going for several years, the same strategy applies: When more net income is needed, put two-thirds of your effort into reducing costs because you can be confident of the results. Put the rest of your effort into improving your marketing.

Most people follow these same practices in their personal life. They put the bulk of their discretionary income into secure forms of financial investment, especially if their equity in a home is counted. They reserve a much smaller amount for high-return, high-risk investments. So choose the known risk over the unknown for the bulk of your effort.

Putting this rule into practice is often easier said than done. Many people who come to us for advice view spending money and time on getting new customers as certain to bring results. "My friend in direct mail assures me that with a 10,000-piece mailing for $8,000, I can get four hundred new customers worth $35,000 in revenue. How can I pass that up?" argues our typical client.

"Not so!" we reply. "Working longer hours to save the costs of a part-time helper and putting $3,000 into a machine that will reduce costs by $4,000 a year will result in a tangible low-risk improvement in net profit."

It is hard for people to see the cost cutting as superior to marketing because they get swept up in the enthusiasm generated by the statistics. But you have direct control over your personal actions, so anything you do to cut costs is low risk and certain to pay off.

Some Arguments Against Bulk Buying

One way to reduce cost, which goes against so-called common sense, is buying smaller quantities. People often look for quantity discounts and buy far more than they can use in a reasonable amount of time. For example, if you were buying a print run for a book you were self-publishing, you might get 10,000 copies for $12,000 or 2,000 copies for $4,000. Because the unit cost for 10,000 is $1.20 as opposed to $2.00 each for $4,000, many people would take the larger quantity, although they have no idea how well the book might sell.

The problem is that, although you could probably sell 2,000 copies of almost any book you published given a few years, you probably couldn't get rid of 10,000 copies of most books without going to the dump. Aside from being out $8,000, you would also have to store the extra books, probably at additonal cost, until you decide to dump them. If the book did sell well, you would have a real number upon which to estimate future sales. If after several smaller print runs you found that sales continued to be strong, then you might consider ordering a larger quantity.

Most quantity purchases give you a similar problem. Phone numbers and addresses often change before large quantities of letterhead can be used up. Ballpoint pens often dry out faster than people use them.

The simple rule is: Don't buy in bulk!

Gift retailer Nadine Travinsky has a sensible approach. "It's not good to buy too much. You can always reorder. A lot of times you get a break when you order large quantities, and it might work out if you know from past experience that you can sell it all. I keep track of the colors that sell the best, and when I get down to a certain number of sweatshirts in that color, I reorder. Each supplier has a different shipping rate, so you have to keep that in mind in deciding when to reorder. I'm always watching my inventory."

Ways to Cut Overhead

In a one-person business, almost by definition, the main way to keep overhead down is by doing most of the work yourself. It's probably impossible to do absolutely everything yourself, so you will turn to others from time to time. Occasionally you will use a lawyer or part-time clerical help; or you may subcontract with an accountant or bookkeeper or a graphic artist. Your goal, however, is to streamline all operations so that you can do most of the work with a minimum of effort. After that, you focus on reducing overhead costs.

As Barbara Johnson points out in her book, *Private Consulting,* there are three areas that are prime candidates for cutting overhead: business space, supplies, and hired services. Working from home is one of the most popular strategies for saving on space costs. To cut costs on work space outside the home, try to locate in older or lower-rent parts of town, or arrange to share space with others who do similar kinds of work. Shared space can help lower the costs of phone, copy machine, and other office equipment as well. Office supplies bear watching too: By keeping an eagle eye on wastage of supplies, you can realize significant savings. Using only temporary services or subcontractors will help you reduce your hired services costs even more than using a part-time employee.

Accountant Malcolm Ponder is a perfect example of this kind of cost management. "One of the things that enables me to make a living charging a third of what other accountants do is that I don't have an office that I have to rent, and I don't hire anyone other than my secretary, who is seasonal. I have almost no overhead, and overhead is what kills most one-person businesses—or makes them kill themselves just to stay a little bit ahead."

SOURCES OF WORKING CAPITAL

Capital is another word for financing your business. Every small business needs a working capital reserve to cover slow periods or to buy inventory in advance of sales. It may also need longer-term capital for the purchase of equipment. To finance a one-person business you can reduce expenses, both business and personal, so there is less of a need to generate as much profit. You can use your personal savings, borrow from friends and family, borrow from your credit cards, and use credit from suppliers. Limited partnerships are another option. Bank loans, credit union loans, and borrowing on the cash value of insurance are also used, but rarely. Many of these forms of financing are used concurrently.

Controlling business expenses was covered earlier in this chapter. Reducing personal expenses is usually a matter of getting a roommate, cutting up charge cards, not buying on credit, and not eating out.

After the first couple of years of running your business you may have no savings left. In that case, you will need to find other sources of capital. If you do have savings, though, your business may be one of the best places to put it.

Both reducing expenses and investing in the business are preferable to borrowing money from someone else. Either strategy keeps the cost of doing business lower because you don't have interest to pay or principal to repay. Moreover, if you haven't borrowed and you decide to stop doing business, you can whenever you wish. You won't need to consider the effect on people to whom you owe money, because there won't be any.

Loans

Sometimes, though, you have to borrow to keep the business going. Borrowing from friends and relatives is the typical source of outside capital for a one-person business. Some businesses need inventory, and many need capital for equipment or fixtures and for leasehold improvements. We offer three pieces of advice if you have to borrow. First, put the loan agreement in writing. The key elements of the written agreement are: (1) the purpose of the loan, (2) the terms of the loan, (3) an alternative method of repayment in case there is a problem, and (4) a mediation procedure to handle any disagreements. Example follows:

Fig. 3.4   Loan Agreement

P R O M I S S O R Y   N O T E

$2,000   March 30, 1983

I, Claude F. Whitmyer, promise to pay Roger Pritchard, or to his order, the principal sum of TWO THOUSAND DOLLARS, interest free, for the period April 1, 1983 through September 30, 1983.

There is no material security for this note. Instead, I promise to exert all reasonable effort towards paying this note on time. Should this not be possible, I agree, first, to replace this loan with another loan, and second, should this, after every avenue has been explored, not be possible, I agree to work full time at a job until principal and late fee have been paid in full.

In the event that this principal sum is not paid by the due date, there will be a late fee of ONE HUNDRED DOLLARS. Should this event occur, each of us agrees to enter into mediation conducted by Charmian Anderson, Shali Parsons & Michael Phillips, whose joint decision as to resolution shall be binding.

In the event that the mediation is unsuccessful and legal action is commenced to collect this note or any sum due under it, I agree to pay a reasonable sum for attorney's fees, to be fixed by the court.

_____   _____
Claude F. Whitmyer   Roger Pritchard

Date: _____   Date: _____

The inclusion of all these elements in a written loan agreement is intended to keep your friends as friends and to allow you to go to the next family Thanksgiving dinner without feeling like an outcast.

Second, if there is any inventory to be sold, you can give your lender a secured loan agreement in which you repay the loan at the cost of inventory plus a fixed markup (such as ten percent) as you sell it. In this way you repay your borrowing as you sell your inventory, box by box or container by container load.

Third, pay your loans promptly and provide your lenders with up-to-date financial statements on the business. This kind of attention will inspire appreciation for your professionalism. It will give your lenders a feeling of participating in what you are doing, which will stand you in good stead later if you need their help again.

Credit cards such as Visa and MasterCard are easy sources of credit, especially if you received them in the mail unsolicited. However, as great as the temptation may be, it is difficult to justify this kind of borrowing because of the high interest costs. Almost any other source of credit, except the Mafia, is cheaper. If credit cards are a necessary form of financing for you, try to limit your borrowing to the less expensive ones from banks in Arkansas and elsewhere. These charge from about thirteen to fifteen percent as of 1988. Any interest rate above fifteen percent should be avoided.

Limited Partnerships

We know many people who have had difficult or unpleasant experiences with partnerships. As a consequence, we do not recommend partnerships ordinarily. Nonetheless, a limited partnership can sometimes be used as a form of financing for a one-person business. In a limited partnership there are two kinds of partners, the general partners and the limited partners. The general partners make all the business decisions, and the limited partners contribute money with the expectation of receiving some sort of return. Limited partnerships allow others to put money into your business in a form that generates earnings for them if your business does well.

The advantages of a limited partnership are obvious. The business has less debt, and the limited partners can only lose what they have invested because, unlike the general partners, the limited partners have no liability beyond the amount of their investment. The most likely candidates for a limited partnership are friends or relatives who need a tax write-off. A new business may be perfect for them because it usually makes little profit and may even report a loss in the beginning, which they can share as a tax deduction. And if the business fails, the limited partners can also deduct the loss.

Credit from Suppliers

Suppliers lend you money in a couple of ways. First, consignments of inventory are a form of loan. Although you are using the merchandise owned by the vendor, you don't have to pay for it until you sell it. Second, suppliers lend you money when they extend you credit. In many fields, suppliers will offer you long-term credit to buy equipment, and they will give you inventory with 100 percent return provisions and ninety days to pay. Sometimes they start out demanding COD payments, and then change to thirty-day terms after they gain experience with you.

Generally, remember the obvious. Always pay your suppliers on time if you can. If you pay your suppliers late in the present, they may not be available in the future when you really need their help. If you are paying your bills slowly, it helps to send your suppliers a financial statement, a list of your other payables, and a written reason for your payment delays. They will appreciate being kept informed and will often volunteer to help out in ways that you can't anticipate.

Other Loans

Most other borrowing is based on secured loans that are attached to tangible objects. All of the same advice applies. Keeping track of loan payments is ideally done on a card or single sheet of paper for each loan (see the accompanying loan payment record for an example).

Fig. 3.5   Loan Payment Record

LOAN PAYMENT RECORD

Loan from: _____

Starting Date: _____   Starting Balance: _____

DATE	CHECK NO.	AMOUNT	BALANCE

Fig. 3.6   Cash Flow Analysis

```
CASH FLOW ANALYSIS FROM INCOME & EXPENSES
LIVING LIGHTLY
First Six Months, 1981
```

	JAN	FEB	MAR	APR	MAY	JUN	YTD
INCOME							
Housewares	10,546	7,950	3,681	6,859	5,460	9,053	43,549
Hardware	18,601	8,056	6,766	6,452	9,236	8,450	57,561
Books	1,295	1,172	1,158	1,515	1,387	1,647	8,174
Non-taxable	536	906	1,025	732	743	843	4,785
TOTAL RETAIL	30,978	18,084	12,630	15,558	16,826	19,993	114,069
COOP PURCHASES SOLD TO OTHERS	2,292	443	917	1,662	832	847	6,993
TOTAL SALES	33,270	18,527	13,547	17,220	17,658	20,840	121,062
Returns & Allowances	1,298	22	54	20	107	392	1,893
NET SALES	31,972	18,505	13,493	17,200	17,551	20,448	119,169
COST OF GOODS SOLD	16,077	7,724	7,145	7,029	7,315	11,177	56,467
GROSS PROFIT	15,895	10,781	6,348	10,171	10,236	9,271	62,702
EXPENSES							
Advertising	552	1,749	314	431	675	551	4,272
Auto & Truck	381		231	122			734
Dues & Publications		18	129		29		176
Education					550		550
Employee Benefits			139	9	640		788
Casual Labor	75			6	7	302	390
Freight Out	185	224	39	76	189	19	732
General Supplies			158	610	148		916
Insurance			453		457	226	1,136
Interest				288	48		336
Legal & Accounting			1,250	175	24		1,449
Office Expense	14	352	328	193	4	106	997
Payroll Taxes	1,600	2,200	1,900	1,851	2,322	1,721	11,594
Postage	21	70	22	11	3		127
Professional Fees			404	157	160	45	766
Store Rent		1,500	1,500	3,000		1,500	7,500
Warehouse Rent			450	900		450	1,800
Outreach & Promotion	280	385	795	705	219	150	2,534
Samples & Demonstrations					48		48
Telephone	389	326	366	270	245	218	1,814
Travel & Entertainment	250	194	437	40	152	79	1,152
Utilites		384	140	124	290	170	1,108
Wages	4,461	6,061	5,403	5,334	6,810	4,764	32,833
TOTAL EXPENSES	8,208	13,463	14,458	14,302	13,020	10,301	73,752
NET PROFIT	7,687	(2,682)	(8,110)	(4,131)	(2,784)	(1,030)	(11,050)
CUMULATIVE PROFIT	7,687	5,005	(3,105)	(7,236)	(10,020)	(11,050)	
GROSS SALES, PROJECTED	25,000	20,000	15,200	30,800	39,500	28,400	158,900
GROSS SALES, ACTUAL	31,972	18,505	13,493	17,200	17,551	20,448	119,169
GROSS PROFIT, PROJECTED	14,000	11,200	8,512	10,920	10,400	9,960	64,992
GROSS PROFIT, ACTUAL	15,895	10,781	6,348	10,171	10,236	9,271	62,702
EXPENSES, PROJECTED	9,250	7,400	5,624	11,470	11,470	11,470	56,684
EXPENSES, ACTUAL	8,208	13,463	14,458	14,302	13,020	10,301	73,752
NET PROFIT, PROJECTED	1,250	600	(152)	(550)	(1,070)	(1,510)	(1,432)
NET PROFIT, ACTUAL	7,687	(2,682)	(8,110)	(4,131)	(2,784)	(1,030)	(11,050)
CUMULATIVE PROFIT (LOSS), PROJECTED	1,250	1,850	1,698	1,148	78	(1,432)	4,592
CUMULATIVE PROFIT (LOSS), ACTUAL	7,687	5,005	(3,105)	(7,236)	(10,020)	(11,050)	(18,719)

CASH FLOW PROJECTIONS

Cash flow is the term used to describe the pattern of all money coming into and going out of your business. A well-managed business always uses a cash flow projection to make decisions about how and when to spend money, and how and when to cut costs. Sometimes the projection can be a simple budget; at other times a more complete chart of income and expenses on a month-by-month basis is needed. The illustration on the facing page shows what a cash flow projection might look like.

Business advisor Paul Terry handles income, expense, and cash flow regularly, relying on this information to keep track of how his business is doing. "I have a business checking account and a manual single entry bookkeeping system. I have not computerized my bookkeeping system, except that once a year I do financial projections on my Vector for the four or five income categories that I have and the ten or fifteen expense categories. I also have allocations for taxes and projects, so I can see what income I might expect and then track it on a monthly basis.

"I need to make a certain amount of income every month. I ask myself questions about whether I am going to make that amount or not, who it's coming from, what's the frequency of repeat, etc. Looking at the income ledger and getting that kind of information is something I do at least monthly, if not more often.

"Expense categories make income tax preparation very simple because everything is up to date by the end of the year. Every month, I bill about a half-dozen clients, so I have a system where I send out an invoice, keep a copy of it, and when the payment comes in, check the copy as having been paid. I'm always very current on who owes me money and very rarely get stuck not getting paid. It's happened twice, and it was due to my own lack of skill."

Musician Alicia Bay Laurel uses a cash flow projection whenever her need for cash changes. She gathers the numbers from a simple but elegant tracking system. "I have a calendar, and when someone asks me to do a gig I write down the date, and I write down the amount of money I'm going to be paid with a little circle around it. Then if the event comes off as scheduled and I make the money, I take my pink highlighter and put a pink dot over that circle. At the end of each month I know exactly what days I played and how much I made on each day. Every three months I pay my quarterly excise taxes. I take my calculator and go through my records for the past three months, add them up, and pay my four percent. In addition I pay state taxes and personal income taxes.

"As far as my business expenses are concerned, I have an accordion file that is broken down into musical instruments, car repair, and so on. As the receipts or canceled checks come in, I put them in this file. At the end of the year when I'm doing my income taxes, I can go through each section and total it up. That's how I do my finances.

"If I'm in a period where my cash needs are greater than usual, I write down everything about my financial situation. This includes what I have in the bank;

everything I have in cash; a list of all the upcoming gigs and what I can expect to make from them; and the money that I'm owed. Then I make a list of all the expenses that I have and prioritize them. These are things that have to be paid right away as well as things that I feel I can buy next month or in two months. This way I have a picture of everything. Then I can say, maybe I don't really need to make that purchase, etc. From a sheet like this I can get an idea of how to allot my money for the coming period of time."

BUDGETING

A budget differs from a cash flow projection in describing how much your *expenses* should be. The cash flow projection describes *when* you expect the money to be coming in and going out. A budget is based on facts. A cash flow projection includes your guesses and calculations based on a set of "what if" assumptions about how you would like to see the business do. You project how much your expenses will be, given your assumptions and how much you will need to make in order to cover them and make a profit. Then you compare what actually happens with what your projection says, month by month (or weekly or quarterly). Budgeting, on the other hand, involves setting the amount you intend to spend on each expense category, and then trying to stick to it.

It is vitally important to have both a cash flow projection and a budget. You need both to keep spending in line and to anticipate future cash flow needs as well as the effects of increases and decreases in volume.

As an example of anticipated cash flow needs, let's look at a therapist who receives half of her income from insurance payments that arrive three months after the treatment. She would want to anticipate the effects of a larger volume of insurance-billed clients. If a twenty percent increase in such clients in a two-month period required an expansion to an adjacent office space costing $1,000 per month more, plus a $3,000 deposit, there might well be a cash shortage, after the rent and deposit were paid, while she waited the three months to receive the insurance payments.

Assume further that because of the anticipated volume change, the therapist needed new office equipment and telephone extensions. A rough calculation might show that the new space wouldn't pay for itself unless the increase in clients was thirty percent and was expected to be permanent. In this case it might be better for her to work longer hours, and on weekends, until she was confident that the higher volume was reliable and until the insurance payments had begun to roll in.

Some one-person businesses have such simple records of income and expense that their owners can carry the relevant figures in their heads, never needing to write them down. If they have been in business a long time, they may feel comfortable with this rather intuitive approach.

We recommend, however, that you always write down the figures that you have projected in your head. Writing material down is a way to keep yourself honest. It is too easy to misremember that you expected $5,000 in July when in your mental projection you really expected $6,000. So when you actually receive $5,500, instead of doing better than you expected, you may have done worse. With expenses, lapses of memory are even more likely. At the beginning of the year you expected expenses to average $43 per client by year-end; by November, however, you think you calculated that it would be $47, which is closer to the actual figure. So you're doing worse than you expected but you don't even realize it. In our experience, when written records are compared to recollections, recollections are invariably inaccurate.

We know of only one circumstance in which a written budget may not be needed. You can probably do budgeting in your head if you have a service business and you have less than four variable expenses (phone, fuel, utilities, repair costs, etc.). Anything more is beyond what human memory can manage, since we can remember only three or four abstractions at a time. Written records allow us to remember much more and with much greater accuracy.

Another reason for a written budget or cash flow projection is that you can use it when getting outside support and advice from peers and friends (*see Figure 3.1*). Your peers and supporters can use your budget and your cash flow projection as a starting point to ask questions about the way your business is developing. Someone might ask, "John, your budget shows that by this month you expected $3,300 a month in revenue from twelve clients and a variable cost per client of $42, but revenues are $3,000 from fourteen clients with an average cost of $55. Do you know why? And does this projection still reflect the way you want to run your business?" This kind of question is useful, and it depends on having a written budget or projection. If your supporters and advisors can see what your expectations and goals were, they can be much more helpful when you need to evaluate your current situation.

Furthermore, they can provide needed emotional support. "The $4,200 in revenue last month is wonderful, Susan, especially since costs were below budget. Congratulations! Keep up the good work!"

RESOURCES

Understanding Financial Information
The Businessman's Information Guide (New York: American Institute of Certified Public Accountants). Order Department, 1211 Avenue of the Americas, New York, NY 10036; 212-575-6200.

John A. Tracy, *How to Read a Financial Report* (New York: John Wiley & Sons, 1983).

Contracts
Stephen Elias, *Make Your Own Contract* (Berkeley, California: Nolo Press, 1987).

Fee Setting
Howard L. Shenson, *The Successful Consultant's Guide to Fee Setting* (Glenelg, Maryland: Bermont Books, 1986).

Consulting
Barbara L. Johnson, *Private Consulting* (Englewood Cliffs, New Jersey: Prentice-Hall, 1982).

4

Information Management

One of our objectives in this book is to reduce the amount of time you spend handling and storing information, and to make the doing of the actual work more fun. Organizing how information flows through your business might seem unimportant when you have so many other things to do. But the more organized you are, the less time you will need to spend tracking and retrieving the information needed to manage the business. It's well worth your effort to develop office systems that smoothly and efficiently separate the wheat from the chaff.

Of course you will not be satisfied if you have lots of information but much of it is trivial. Your goal is to handle all of the information coming into your business with the greatest effectiveness and the least effort. This includes incoming information from clients or customers, such as appointment requests, orders, and questions that need answering.

MAIL

The traditional advice is still good: Open the mail near a trash can, and never touch a piece of paper twice. You can handle any piece of mail either immediately or later. Most mail can be handled immediately; you can either throw it away or put it in a file. It is not an immediate response, though, if the file you put it in is labeled "to do later."

Some mail requires thought over time, but that's rare. The main reason for any delay in an immediate response is lack of time. Sometimes the proper response may depend on something else, such as more information. Another good reason to delay is that answering mail in a batch may be more efficient.

The most efficient way of handling mail in a one-person business is to assign a time to do it and not open the mail until then. Sit next to a trash can and near a desk with the appropriate action files. Label these action files with descriptors that make sense to you. For instance, you might put mail that needs more information into a file called "more info." Mail that can be filed could go into "file." And mail that can be handled during slow times, or all at once one day a week, could be put into a file labeled "batch." Mail that needs immediate attention can go into "answer now."

Any mail in "Answer Now" can be responded to by writing directly on the original letter and keeping a photocopy. This is a quick way to answer mail, it is efficient, and in some situations it is perfectly acceptable. Trade standards and good personal judgment will help you determine whether it's appropriate. It is much like the stock two-way letter form you can buy in any office supply store. But some people feel that even these are rude, so think twice before using this time-saving trick.

Jack, who makes and sells handmade rocking chairs, sorts his mail into "new orders," "information requests," and "customer mail." The new orders get an immediate reply plus a work order with time estimate that goes back with the confirmation. The information requests go into a pile near the coffeepot where they are kept in the order received and handled randomly during phone conversations and idle moments. The customer mail is taken home for thoughtful, caring replies, which Jack does with his wife during evenings and weekends.

Unwanted Mail

When you are in business for yourself, and you have reached a stage of development marked by moderate success and regular work or sales, you will probably begin to notice the phenomenon of unwanted mail. This is mail that you receive because someone you don't know, from somewhere you never heard of, has heard about you or your product and decides to write. Unwanted mail is generally from well-meaning people who have mistakenly written to you because of an affinity they feel for what you are doing or selling. It is unwanted because their query doesn't really pertain to what you are doing, or it would be better answered by some other person or business.

Early on in your business you don't think much about these letters, and you just answer them when and in the best way you can. But later, as you become more successful or better known, the volume can begin to be greater than you can justifiably handle without taking away from the effective operation of your business. What to do about it is not an easy question to answer. One solution is to create standard replies that are preprinted or photocopied when needed. This allows you to batch the unwanted mail and answer it at your convenience. Your stock reply could contain some suggestions about where the inquirer might look for answers. After you have handled a few batches, you will know what the most frequently asked questions are, and you can create a form letter with all of the answers on one page and boxes next to them. Then just check the right answers before mailing the form letters out.

Old Mail

Both ordinary and unwanted mail can sometimes stack up. When you are too busy to answer because of the pressures of current work demands, the stacks may begin to age. How old is too old? This will vary a lot, depending on the contents of individual letters. You will have to make careful judgments about every piece. Generally, though, with requests for information that are more than two months old and that have not been repeated, the chances are good that your answer is no longer needed. You may want to apologize, or you may judge that it isn't really important, in which case there is nothing to do. If you are like us, just reading this paragraph will make you uneasy. The best prevention is to avoid letting your mail fall behind. The best solution is to develop the attitude that it's all right to toss some of it in the first place.

DAILY RECORDS

Of particular importance to good information management are the phone log, activity record, and meeting record. These three systems help you monitor how you spend your time, and they keep you from letting important tasks and agreements go undone, which is a danger if you have them logged only in your head.

Phone Log

A phone log allows you to keep track of who is calling you, why they called, and whether you have gotten back to them. It can also help you track any toll or long distance calls so that you can get reimbursed, if appropriate. Here is an example of a phone log that works.

Fig. 4.1   Phone Log

PHONE LOG			
DATE:		PAGE:	
WHO CALLED	PHONE (S)	WHAT THEY WANTED	DISPOSITION

DISPOSITION: D = Done - Dr = Dropped - Msg = Message Left - P = Pending

Activity Record

An activity record allows you to track how you spend your time. Any one-person business can benefit from a diary of this sort because it can be used as the basis for making decisions about time management. To businesses that bill for their time it is of particular importance. It also serves as what the IRS calls a "contemporaneous record," which can be used to document the validity of your travel mileage, meals, entertainment, and other business expenses at tax time. The minimum information includes date, purpose, who was present, and the number of miles traveled or dollars spent. If you use a pocket calendar for your diary, the date is there already, so you have less to write. Also, many pocket calendars have a small table printed in a corner of each page, already set up for expenses so that all you have to do is fill in the blanks.

Fig. 4.2   Activity Record

ACTIVITY RECORD

PROJECT -- CLIENT:		

Type:
1. Mail   4. Visit
2. Phone   5. Other_____
3. Computer 6. Other_____

Contact Persons:
A:
B:
C:

Type	Date	Notes	Time Start	Stop	Elapsed

Meeting Record

Recording your meetings is important for much the same reason as recording your other activities. However, recording meeting information may require more room than a pocket calendar allows, so always have extra paper available. Write down the date, purpose, and who was present. In addition, it's a good idea to record the agenda, or list of what was discussed at the meeting; topics to be discussed at any follow-up meetings; when and where these meetings will take place; and what the various attendees have agreed to do as a result of the current meeting, or in preparation for the next. Here is an example of a form that you could use to save writing time:

Fig. 4.3 Meeting Log

MEETING LOG

Reference: ____________ Date: ________ Hour: ________ Place: ____________

PARTICIPANTS: | AGENDA:

DECISIONS, CONCLUSIONS, ACTIONS TAKEN OR ADVISED:

AGENDA FOR NEXT MEETING: (Date,Location,Items)

NOTES:

FILES

A good filing system helps you organize two kinds of information: the kind you use daily, and need to be able to get your hands on quickly; and the kind you refer to only once in a while. It's also important to keep the sheer volume of files manageable by systematically discarding records that are no longer essential to your business.

For ongoing business activities you need an effective system to keep track of all the paper each project generates. Your system should organize activities and projects, clients or customers, prospects, and general management information. Obviously the faster you can retrieve information from your files, the more efficient you will be.

Most people have some way of filing their business records, which very often consists primarily of manila file folders stuck in a file drawer. Although it looks neat and tidy on the outside, chaos often reigns inside.

If this describes your filing system, we may have just the system for you. It's called the "fat-file" system. It is very easy, especially in the beginning, because you start with just one file folder and put everything into it. In creating your fat-file filing system you can use any of the many kinds of folders that are available today from office supply stores and mail-order companies. You can use a manila folder, hanging folder, or even an expandable accordion type, letter or legal size. The important thing is that the look and feel match your aesthetic sense and make it fun to use. Color helps, and file folders come in a wide variety of colors.

As soon as your first folder becomes so full that it takes more than five minutes to find what you are looking for, you create a second folder. Now it is necessary to label both folders so that you know what each contains. You could simply divide them up alphabetically, with *A-L* in one folder and *M-Z* in another. Or you could use a numbering system or file by date received, and so forth. Label them in whatever way is personally meaningful to you.

After many years of trying out different systems, Claude has come up with a simple one that groups all information about ongoing activities into four categories: clients, accounting and fiscal, promotion and future work, and mailing and phone lists. The fattest files are in the category of accounting and fiscal, where all the bookkeeping and tax records are kept. The client files are pretty fat too, containing documents, notes, and materials on every project for every client in the past two years. Records on clients for whom no work has been done in the past two years are kept filed away in a box in the storage closet. The file for promotion and future work contains such marketing information as ideas for newsletters, testimonials from happy clients, and thoughts and plans about future work. The file for mailing and phone lists contains business cards, change of address notices that need to be entered into the Rolodex, copies of mailing lists, and the telephone numbers of all clients, prospects, and suppliers, etc. These four files cover eighty percent of Claude's storage of ongoing information, and have grown into a couple of drawers full of records over the past several years, necessitating the creation of subcategories within each. But because the fat-file principle has been maintained, it still never takes longer than five minutes to find an old piece of information when it is needed.

Reference Files

Reference files contain information that you may want occasionally but for which you have no regular need. If you find that you are retrieving something less than once or twice a month, it probably belongs in a reference file. You might start such a file, for example, to hold a wish list of books or magazine subscriptions that you want to buy when your cash flow allows. Or to keep clippings of information on a topic or field of ideas that interests you. Other items such as maps and recreation or travel information, photos, slides, or tapes also fit in the category of reference material.

The simplest storage solution is to buy a few sturdy cardboard boxes, such as the archive boxes manufactured by Bankers Box and used by attorneys for storing records. These are just the right dimensions to hold either letter or legal sized files, and they are strong enough to stack three or four high. Just be sure to label them clearly on the outside so that you can quickly find the box you need.

Plans and Dreams

Another important part of information organization is to also keep your plans and dreams fresh and accessible. Filing them away in the back of a file drawer is like filing them in the back of your mind, where they can be forgotten.

We recommend reserving wall space for them, where you can pin up a planning calendar, vacation ideas, or notes and drawings about long-range projects. In this way your plans and dreams will be right in front of you. Another idea is to put a notebook right next to your bed, so it is easy to review your long-range goals just before falling asleep.

Labeling for Keeps—Or Is It?

What was life like before 3M Post-it Notes? They come in numerous sizes, colors, and formats, and their uses are almost too many to count. But a note of caution from personal experience: Don't use a Post-it to label anything that you want to stay labeled. As a means of labeling boxes slated for long-term record storage, Post-its just won't work. You don't want to go into your storage closet to retrieve a record, and find a pile of Post-It Notes lying on the floor in front of your boxes. Nor do you want it to be easy for someone else to remove a label accidentally. Post-its were designed for temporary labeling. They have an adhesive backing with low tack, and it weakens with time. For long-lasting labels, write directly on the box or use a "permanent" label stock available from most stationery stores.

Actively cultivating long-range plans and dreams creates a "big picture" context and a higher level of motivation to do the day-to-day tasks necessary for your long-term success as a businessperson.

Discarding

Discarding is an important and often overlooked record-keeping task. It consists of systematically putting into the garbage everything that you no longer need to run your business. It is easy to throw away junk mail or information that has outlived its usefulness, such as old magazines or letters. You must be careful, however, in deciding what financial information to discard and when. You will need many of your financial documents if you are ever audited by federal or state tax agencies, which can require you to defend your tax statements for several back years. Other records may be needed if you are ever sued; some of these must be kept up to seven years. Capital gains records need to be held for the period of the gain.

To know how long to keep your various records, check with your accountant or lawyer if you use one. Or you might get a discarding booklet prepared by a company that manufactures filing supplies or shredders. These booklets contain tables of recommended retention periods. They are available at many office supply stores or from the manufacturer.

TELEPHONE

For the majority of one-person businesses, the phone is the main source of information transactions. It is wise to apply some control to the timing of incoming calls, but how much is a matter of personal taste and style.

In our society it is common practice not to accept most calls between 9:00 P.M. and 8:00 A.M. Because of the differences in time zones, some businesses on the West Coast start at 6:00 A.M. in order to match the East Coast opening time of 9:00 A.M. And businesses that have overseas customers sometimes work late at night. Customs also differ by trade. Politicians call each other until midnight, farmers start early in the morning.

You can control the timing of incoming phone calls by creative use of the phone and answering machine. The following examples show different ways of using a phone to good advantage:

- Doug, a theater director, has one tape that takes messages but that also refers callers to two other tapes that answer the two most common phone questions.
- Sara, a graphic artist, has two separate phone lines. One she always answers because it is for primary working clients; the other has a tape for inquiries and return calls.

- Carol, a production weaver, wants diversions, so she has a headset on her phone and answers the phone whenever it rings. She talks as she works, with both hands free. At night or when she is away, she turns on the answering machine.
- Tom, a tile setter, is often out in the field, so he phones his machine every two hours, when he usually needs a break anyway.

Michael Phillips does a lot of his work on the phone. Because he receives so many phone calls, it is efficient for him to separate his calls into certain categories:

1. Inquiries he can handle by an automatic mail response.
2. Prospect calls, which are arranged in the order received. When he's in an up mood he can call all of them at one time.
3. Friends outside of business. When Michael wants a pleasant diversion, he can return these calls.
4. Ongoing clients, whom he has told to expect return calls between 4:00 P.M. and 6:00 P.M. unless they ask otherwise.
5. All other calls. These he batches to make at one time, with a note describing what they are about. These calls include people he doesn't want to talk to because they want something inappropriate or because they contacted him by mistake. (Having a record of resources and people he can refer others to is helpful in these cases.)

Phone Features

In most major metropolitan areas there are three useful features that can be added to your phone: call forwarding, three-way calling, and call waiting.

When you are going to be away from your normal place of business, you can use call forwarding to send your calls to any phone you choose. Three-way calling allows you to add a third person to any in-progress phone conversation without the help of the operator. Call waiting gives a signal when you are on the line and another caller is trying to reach you. It enables you to put the first caller on hold, answer the second call, and then return to your original call. You can shift back and forth between the two calls as often as you wish.

Without question, call forwarding and three-way calling will make your life easier, but call waiting is controversial. Its advocates argue that it keeps them from missing important calls. Its critics argue that it is rude—like telling someone who is meeting with you that the next person to come in is more important.

If you choose to have call waiting, you might make some rules for yourself that become easier with practice. First, train yourself never to give the second caller priority, no matter how strong the temptation may be. When you hear the interrupt signal, gracefully ask the current party to hold for a moment. Pick up the incoming call and tell the caller that you are on another call and will have to call back. Go right back to the first party as quickly as possible. Aim at no more than thirty seconds from putting the first party on hold to coming back to them. Be sure to call the second party back as you promised. Paul Rosenblum, a fund-raising consultant for nonprofit organizations, uses this approach and word of his courtesy has spread. Most of the reactions are favorable because of his consistent use of this approach.

You can also handle call waiting by installing a second phone line with the cheapest possible service. Most phone companies refer to this as "pots" or plain old telephone service. Hook up an inexpensive phone machine to that line with a short outgoing message such as, "I'm on the other line. Leave your name and number and I'll call you right back." Then use your call forwarding service to put your regular line on call forwarding to your second line. You can still call out on your first line, even when it is in the call forwarding mode. The main difference between this solution and the previous one is that people whom you call never experience being put on hold. Its drawbacks are (1) it is more expensive, and (2) if someone calls you right after you have hung up from a call but before you have taken the first line off call forwarding, you cannot answer.

A few telephone companies also offer a service called delayed call forwarding, which could handle this second drawback. Delayed call forwarding allows the phone to ring two to four times before the forwarding feature activates, giving you time to pick up the phone if you wish to.

Ultimately, the decision to have call waiting or not must be made by how you feel about it. As with all the systems you use, pay constant attention to the feedback you get from your clients, customers, or suppliers. If you get any negative reactions, change what you're doing.

Answering Machine or Answering Service?

Another controversial question for one-person businesses is whether to have an answering machine or an answering service. You will definitely need one or the other to stay in business, because you cannot always answer the phone when it should be answered. Even if you are at the phone all day, it's a good idea to be available to your customers at night as well, even if only on a machine. Customers will appreciate being able to call and find out your hours and location, or place an order or leave a question. A phone that rings and rings, no matter what the hour, does not instill confidence.

Answering services have been readily available for over thirty years, and as they have become more affordable, they have helped support the growth of one-person businesses. But as inexpensive answering machines have become available in the last five years, they have contributed to a regular boom in one-person businesses. There is little an answering service can do that an answering machine cannot. A major plus of an answering machine is that it is cheaper than a service. A typical machine with all the features needed sells for less than $100. A typical answering service costs $10 to $15 per month at a minimum and more if you want twenty-four-hour service or computer controlled message taking. The life of an answering machine is two to three years. You can do the arithmetic, but the conclusion has to be that an answering machine is more cost-effective than a service. Another point in favor of an answering machine is that you can retrieve your messages or change your outgoing message at any time of day or night. With answering services, you are constrained by the working hours of the service or by your willingness to pay for extended hours.

A major drawback to answering services is that you do not directly control the manner in which your phone is answered. You and your clients can be treated rudely or put abruptly on hold, and all you can do is complain about it afterwards. If you decide on a service, choose it carefully and be prepared to pay more to get prompt, courteous handling of your customer calls.

One thing an answering service can do that an answering machine cannot is make appointments. This ability can be very important to some one-person businesses. If you can find a service willing to do it, you can have the service hold a master calendar for you and book appointments when you are unable to answer the phone.

Salli's massage professional has an answering service that schedules all her appointments. The service is so good at answering calls and handling the bookings that many people assume she has a secretary. An airplane rental company that Michael uses offers a similar courtesy. If you call when no one is in the office, the answering service will make the airplane rental reservation for you so that you don't have to call back.

Michael Stein, a free-lance market researcher, has both an answering service and an answering machine. His machine is a Panasonic two-line model with all the key features, plus an automatic rollover feature so that if the phone rings when someone is recording a message, the machine will redirect the second caller to the message tape for the second line. Mike found that it confused some of his clients if the outgoing message on the second line was different from the message on the first line. But there were enough calls on both lines to live with this problem. Mike uses the answering service if he wants to leave a personalized message for a client. Then no one else has to listen to the personal message, as they would if it were on the machine. The system works this way: The answering machine is set to answer on the second line only. At the same time the answering service is instructed to pick up all calls. When persons for whom there are special messages call, the service gives them the messages. Anyone else is given the choice of leaving a message with the answering service or being forwarded to the answering machine set to pick up calls on the second line. The outgoing message on the machine is simply, "This is voice mail. Leave your message after the beep." There is no need for any identification or explanation because the answering service operator has already done that. This system allows callers to choose whether they want to speak to a person or a machine, effectively handling the machine versus service controversy without offending anyone.

If you have an answering service, call it occasionally to make sure that the operators are doing a good job. Imagine that you are a potential customer, someone who does not know your business. Remember that in many cases the phone is the only way a customer has of judging your business. Try to get to know your regular operators, their supervisors, and the owner of the business on a first-name basis. Send holiday cards, thank-you notes, or flowers once in a while, especially if you have noticed an operator going the extra distance for you.

If you have an answering machine, call your own number periodically to make sure the machine is working properly and the message is coming out the way you expect. Be sure to keep messages up to date.

Most Frequently Asked Questions

You can cut down on telephone time by preparing a list of the questions that are asked most frequently and the answers to them. Then when these questions arise, you will not have to handle them as if they were being asked for the first time. Such a list is also useful if you are sick or on vacation or have someone helping in your office for whatever reason.

If you have lots of inquiries, get a second answering machine that takes variable-length outgoing message tapes, and use it to provide answers to the most frequently asked questions. You will need a second phone line, but it can be basic service at the lowest possible rate. Time how long it takes to speak the answers to the questions you have chosen to automate, and buy an outgoing message tape long enough to record those answers. Put the answers on the tape, and you are in business. But don't forget to mention in the outgoing message of your primary answering machine that it's possible to get answers to frequently asked questions by calling the second number. Also tell your answering service to pass this information along. Then no matter when people call you, even at 3:00 in the morning, they can get some answers.

800 Numbers

Although one-person businesses rarely have an 800 number, it can be useful in a few cases—for example, a mail-order business that wants to encourage phone orders, a software publisher offering a support service for its programs, or any business specializing in selling information. The 800 service can expand your trading arena by allowing customers outside your local calling area to call your business at no charge to them. Whether to get an 800 number is a question of costs and benefits and must be calculated on a case-by-case basis.

In California, for instance, Pacific Bell currently charges $36 per month plus long distance tolls, which are lower with the 800 number than if the customer called collect. For handling customer requests, feedback, and customer service, this can be an inexpensive way to stay on top of how your product or service is perceived and to make sure that customers are satisfied. And once you get your 800 number you are automatically listed with 800 Information (800-555-1212), giving you additional nationwide exposure.

Telephone Courtesy

Many people don't know how to talk courteously on the phone. This sad fact is probably a consequence of phones being a new technology, one for which we have yet to develop widely accepted rules of etiquette. A few pointers will help you establish your reputation as a one-person business that cares about its customers.

First, consider carefully how you answer the phone. Do you pick it up within three or four rings? Do you merely say "hello" when you pick it up? Somehow, from movies or our parents, we have grown up with the idea that "hello" is all that's required. For business purposes, however, "hello" is a waste of time. Callers need to know they have reached the right person, and most won't recognize your voice. Always answer with at least your name, and if you have a company name, give that too.

Second, if you have a hold button, don't use it for more than thirty seconds without coming back on the line to let the caller know you have not forgotten. Nothing irritates a caller more than to be kept waiting with no explanation. Even with an explanation, don't make anyone wait for very long. Arrange to call back with the information, if necessary.

When giving someone a phone number or address over the phone, speak slowly. Separate phone numbers into three parts, the area code, the prefix, and the four-digit number. Say them slowly and clearly into the mouthpiece: four one five (pause) six seven six (pause) eight eight one nine.

When you are receiving a number, wait to hear the whole number before you start repeating it back. Otherwise you may find yourself repeating the first part of the number as your caller is beginning to give the second part. Neither of you will hear what the other said.

The same is true for addresses. Break them down into small parts that are easy to repeat and remember, and speak slowly. You will greatly reduce the number of times you have to repeat what you say. If you are receiving an address, listen carefully and wait until the whole address is given before repeating it back. You should be writing as fast as you can. But you will have plenty of time to make corrections at the end, without having to ask the other person to start over.

RESOURCES

Records Control and Storage Handbook, with Retention Schedules   (Franklin Park, Illinois: Bankers Box). Describes in detail not only when to throw your records out, but also how to keep them in storage until the retention period is over. May be ordered from Bankers Box, 2607 North 25th Avenue, Franklin Park, IL 60131.

V. Stibic, *Personal Documentation for Professionals: Means and Methods*   (New York: North-Holland Publishing Company, 1980). Basic systems for filing books, reports, journals, photocopies, slides and photos, letters, etc.

Stephanie Winston, *Getting Organized*   (New York: Warner Books, 1978). Covers maximizing storage space, reducing shopping time, increasing efficiency, etc.

5

Time Management

Managing your time is the key to structuring your work to suit your lifestyle. The tools described in this chapter will help you to assume control over your time so that you can choose which days of the week to work, for how many hours, and when.

The most often reported barrier to a smoothly functioning, joy-filled business experience is the feeling of having no control over time. There just never seems to be enough hours in the day, or days in the week, to get everything accomplished. But this feeling does not have to go with the territory. With planning you can build a work schedule that accommodates such personal considerations as the time of day you work best, whether you have children, and how much money you need.

Landscape gardener Eileen Mulligan's life is built around her children. "My children are the main organizers of my time. I have to make the house payment and support my children. If the laundry and other chores don't get done, I can live with that as long as I am providing us with a good life. My work and personal life have to balance."

Suzanne Maxson, a job development researcher, has figured out how to take advantage of the flexibility that running her own business gives her. "The beauty of this business is that I have enough freedom to structure the day the way I want to. I'm on the phone with prospective employers beginning at 8:30, and I work until noon. Two afternoons a week I take classes at the local college, but the other days I often return to the office after lunch and spend a few more hours on the phone, which I enjoy doing. In the late afternoon I write my reports. I never try to do this work when I don't feel like it. If I suddenly feel myself tuning out—just staring out the window—I go outside for five minutes. I always feel free to take time away when I need to."

"My highest priority is to provide as much painting time as possible," states Bill Morehouse, fine artist. "This means working without interruption so I can use my best energy and concentration. I'm willing to let all the other things slide—dishes in the sink, social obligations, or whatever. When I'm in New York I settle into a routine. I get up and have my coffee and then work for three hours. Then I'll visit some galleries, have lunch, get my mail, see a friend. Afterwards I come back to my studio and work until evening. Some evenings I'll go to a social function or gallery opening. Sometimes, though, if the work is intriguing enough I'll continue to work into the evening."

BILLABLE VERSUS NONBILLABLE TIME

In a one-person business, more than in any other business, owners find that they have to make better use of their administrative time and be more productive during their periods of peak productivity. All businesses, large or small, have to deal with nonbillable, or administrative time, but in bigger businesses part of the administrative work is handled by others, making it less apparent.

There's not enough time for me to do all the things I have to do.

There are so many trivial things to do and interruptions, I get so frustrated because I can't get the real work done.

These are the two most common statements we hear from one-person business owners. It's worthwhile looking beyond the obvious frustration of these statements to investigate what might really be happening in the business.

The statement about not having enough time to do all the necessary things could come from anyone. Politicians say it, secretaries say it, corporate executives say it. For the owner of a one-person business it usually means: If I could only do more I could run my business better. Actually, if your health is good and you have a lot of enthusiasm for what you do, then you are probably already near capacity in working hours and really don't have more time. The solution is to increase both your efficiency and your effectiveness. The difference between efficiency and effectiveness is this: Efficiency is how well you do things. Effectiveness is getting things done. To increase your efficiency, you must streamline your systems so that more gets done with less effort. To increase your effectiveness, use systems and tools that keep you on track all during the course of your tasks and projects. In this chapter we address both needs.

GOALS AND PRIORITIES

Making the most of your time involves two elements: having explicit goals to enable you to set priorities, and making good schedules so that you can keep your priorities in order. Then when a friend drops by that you want to visit with, and you have to get two more boxes ready for the afternoon mail, you have decided on your priorities in advance. You don't wish you had more time, you know you have to get the work done. So you explain this to your friend and fix another time to get together.

Behind the statement that there are so many interruptions and trivial things to do is the feeling that the productive work you do—what you can bill for—often seems subsidiary to the administrative responsibilities you must perform. The productive work is what it's all about, you think, while administrative work seems like a frustrating interruption. This sentiment is very common among people who are newly self-employed, and rare among those who have been in business for some time. To the old-timers, the distinction between work and interruption is no longer clear. Either the trivia has come to be appreciated for its value, or it has been discarded. In fact, most of what people call trivia is actually the basic administrative work that keeps a business going, and in a one-person business this can represent a very high percentage of time. "Interruptions" turn out to be fundamental to your business. Answering the telephone, sending the mail, buying supplies, and having planning meetings with clients are all important aspects of your work. Experienced people know this, and work with certainty, confidence, and efficiency—the result of blending all the elements of their work.

A photographer like Norman Prince puts in a large amount of administrative time (sometimes as much as eighty percent) to productive time (twenty percent). The administrative time consists of meeting with clients and prospects, talking on the phone, handling mail (including requests for samples of work), getting supplies, doing bookkeeping and other paperwork, and lots of cataloging and filing of past work. The productive time consists of shooting the photos and developing the film. If Norman resented this ratio he would never succeed in his business.

By contrast, a therapist might spend forty percent administrative to sixty percent productive time. In this case the administrative time would include making appointments, keeping records of sessions, bookkeeping and other paperwork, interviewing potential clients, and meeting with other professionals. The productive time is the actual therapy sessions with clients.

Administrative and productive times differ for each type of business. For freelance writers, public speakers, and consultants, two hours of administrative time for every hour of productive time would not be unusual. For gardeners, goldsmiths, and truck drivers, the opposite might be true: one hour of administrative for every two hours of productive. All businesses, big or small, have to deal with administrative time. In bigger businesses, part of the administrative work is handled by others; the rest is dealt with in executive meetings, which makes it seem less trivial.

When you accept the reality of administrative time and its inherent relationship to productive time, you will find yourself taking a different approach to your business. You can begin by patterning your approach after people who have been in business for many years. Experienced businesses have consciously designed their administrative time to be as supportive of their productive time and as efficient as possible, and to be a rewarding, enjoyable part of their business.

Property manager Ted Rabinowitsh probably speaks for a lot of experienced businesspeople when he says, "I'm not comfortable unless I have both time and money elements worked out so that they are clear and under control. What I like is the balance. I enjoy doing the paperwork and I enjoy doing the physical work, but I wouldn't want to have to do either of them exclusively."

TIME MANAGEMENT THEORIES AND PLANNING

There are two views of time that can help you overcome the feeling that there is never enough of it. One is to recognize time for what it really is: something your mind does to describe the inevitability of change. The past and the future are not real because you can never be in the past or the future. The past is a memory record activated in the brain, right now, in the moment of remembering. The future is identical to the past in this respect. It is a plan or fantasy in your mind, right now, as you mentally build it or think about it. Memory and planning (the past and the future) are really just the process of filling in the gaps in presently observable experience, giving you an image of continuous existence.

The only time there is, really, is *right now*. This powerful perspective can help you be fully present in the moment. It can also allow you to ask the empowering question, "What is the best use of my 'time' right now?"

With this question, the other approach to time comes into play. Conscientiously scheduling how you will use your time, including time off, is called time management. Because it is so easy to get caught up in the demands of the day-to-day operation of your business, you can easily neglect time management. But it is one of the most powerful tools a small business person can develop.

Planning is not usually thought of as a time management activity, but it should be. It is useful to divide planning into three primary periods: short-range, mid-range and long-range. Short-range planning covers from the present to six months from now. Mid-range is from six months to two years. Long-range is from two to ten years, and sometimes longer. Although the process of planning for these three periods is roughly identical, naturally the degree of detail and abstraction changes.

Short-Range Planning

Short-range planning is easy with three basic tools: to-do lists, prioritizing, and scheduling. First you write a list of the things you need to get done. Next

Fig. 5.1   To Do List

```
TO DO LIST:
---------------------------------------------------------------------------
¡ Disposition ¡ Stress ¡ Priority ¡ Description                           ¡
---------------------------------------------------------------------------
              ¡        ¡          ¡
_____
              ¡        ¡          ¡
_____
              ¡        ¡          ¡
_____
              ¡        ¡          ¡
_____
              ¡        ¡          ¡
_____
              ¡        ¡          ¡
_____
              ¡        ¡          ¡
_____
              ¡        ¡          ¡
_____
              ¡        ¡          ¡
_____
              ¡        ¡          ¡
_____
              ¡        ¡          ¡
_____
              ¡        ¡          ¡
_____
              ¡        ¡          ¡
_____
              ¡        ¡          ¡
_____
              ¡        ¡          ¡
_____
              ¡        ¡          ¡
_____
              ¡        ¡          ¡
_____
              ¡        ¡          ¡
_____
              ¡        ¡          ¡
_____
              ¡        ¡          ¡
_____
              ¡        ¡          ¡
_____
              ¡        ¡          ¡
_____
              ¡        ¡          ¡
_____
              ¡        ¡          ¡
_____
              ¡        ¡          ¡
_____
              ¡        ¡          ¡
_____
              ¡        ¡          ¡
_____
              ¡        ¡          ¡
_____
DISPOSITON:  D = Done  -  DR = Dropped  -  P = Passed On  -  W = Waiting for info
```

you rank them so that the most important items will get done first. Finally, using a calendar, you schedule when you will do them.

To-Do Lists To-do lists can be written on anything, on paper (in a notebook or on the wall), on a blackboard, or in a computer. Most people find it easy to come up with a sizable to-do list in, say, ten or fifteen minutes. You are seldom unaware of what to do next; getting it done is the problem.

Your to-do list will be doubly helpful if you reserve some space on the left side of your paper or blackboard to write the disposition of each item—that is, the answer to the question: What have I done with this item? One method, shown in the following illustration, uses a set of symbols for the four most common dispositions: pending, done, given to someone else, and dropped. In our example, the absence of a symbol means "pending," a check mark means "done," an arching right arrow means "given to someone else," and a down arrow means "dropped." Any symbols can be used that make sense to you. Experts in time management offer this tip: Instead of the negative act of crossing out an item, reward yourself with a few kind words, written next to each item as you complete it. Positive, reinforcing words like "good work," "well done," "great" are fine. It may seem silly at first, but like the grade-school star system it still feels good, and many people find it more motivating than simply crossing out a completed item.

Prioritizing We recommend two effective methods of prioritizing and suggest you try both to see which one suits you best. The first is Alan Lakein's "ABC method." In *How to Get Control of Your Time and Your Life* (New York: New American Library, 1973), Alan suggests that you sort all to-do's into three categories: *A*, "for urgent, must get done right away," *B*, "very important, must eventually get done," and *C*, "important, should do when can." You do the *A*s, put the *B*s in a drawer until you can get to them, and throw the *C*s away.

Another method we have tried (but can't remember where we found it) is the "Priority/Stress Level" method illustrated below. With this method, you classify all your to-do's into *A*s, *B*s, and *C*s, as with Lakein's method. But you go one step further and also classify them into *1*s, *2*s, and *3*s, according to how stressful they are. *A* will be the most important, and *3* will be the most stressful. The method works by completing your to-do's in the order of most important, least stressful. In other words, do the *A1*s first, then the *A2*s, *A3*s, *B1*s, etc. The theory is that by doing the important things that you feel the most comfortable with first (*A1*s), you will be more productive and will feel more of a sense of accomplishment. The things you are best at will offer you the least stress. When you do important but not so stressful tasks, you will not only accomplish a lot, you will also get more done than if you wrestled with the things you're not good at, no matter how important they are (*see Figure* 5.2).

Scheduling After listing and prioritizing the things you need to do, you must set aside the time to actually get the most important of them done. This is critical

Fig. 5.2   Prioritized To Do List

THINGS TO DO
TODAY

DATE _____

✓		PRIORITY

FOLLOW-UP

THINGS TO DO
TODAY

DATE: 10/20/88

✓		PRIORITY
✓	Finish corrections of Chs 1-5	A3
✓	Drop off to designer	A2
	Do Query letter to "Computer Currents"	A1
	Calls:	
	Black Mountain re: water & COA	B3
→	Kat	B3
↓	Gilbert to make appointment	A3

FOLLOW-UP

because when we are busy, we sometimes forget to set aside the hour per week it might take to do the bookkeeping, or the thirty minutes a day needed for making marketing calls, and so forth.

Calendars Calendars are indispensable tools for scheduling and short-range planning. There are basically two kinds: those that go in a notebook and those that go on the wall. It works best to use only one calendar to keep track of the immediate future. With two, it becomes difficult to reconcile the information on them. A large wall calendar has the advantage of keeping your schedule, larger than life, right before your eyes. This is the best choice if most of your work is done in your office and you seldom need to visit clients or customers. The few times you need to jot down an appointment and happen to be away from your calendar, a small pocket notebook or piece of paper should suffice until you can transfer it to the wall calendar. If, however, you are on the road or in clients' offices most of the time, then a good notebook calendar is essential.

Month-at-a-Glance Calendars Notebook calendars come in a variety of sizes and layouts—from pocket size to 8-1/2 by 11 inches, and from one or two days per page to a week or month per page. Although any of these is suitable for noting your day-to-day commitments and appointments, the month per page is the most helpful. It provides a perspective on the near future that will help you stay in touch with your work load. Because you can accurately see what is going on, you can more easily spread the work load across a reasonable period of time. This will help you avoid becoming overloaded.

Custom satchel designer Teri Joe Wheeler agrees. "One of my biggest breakthroughs this year is that I decided to carry around a regular calendar. It's just the ordinary kind that hangs on everyone's wall. But it folds in half, and I can slip it into my bag. Those engagement calendars that show you a week at a time don't work for me. I need to see the whole month at once."

Notebook Calendars

In the past two years the availability of good pocket calendars has grown phenomenally. This is directly related to the growth in one-person and other small businesses, and it has created a boom in the office supplies industry. You can visit almost any office supply store and find some kind of notebook calendar that will meet your personal needs. Of the brands available in office supply stores, Day Runner and Record Plate have a wider than usual choice in pages, permitting you to customize your system. Quo Vadis also has a good variety of hardbound book calendars that are especially designed for clergy, doctors, or other professionals. You may be able to adapt one of these to your needs. Day Timers, available through mail-order, offers a wide choice of pages and binders and is reasonably priced.

Three- to Four-Month Calendars Another helpful time management tool is a chart you make yourself, covering three or four months at a time, that serves to remind you of future promises and plans. You can post your regular monthly meetings, holiday and vacation schedule, other planned time off, and so forth. It is especially important to have this kind of calendar if your business is seasonal, if you are a manufacturer, or if you give lectures, workshops, and seminars. In these types of business you must promise performance well before the delivery day, and without this chart you run the risk of overcommitting yourself or of making promises without taking your long-range goals into consideration. This tool is also helpful in planning your marketing schedule because you can see when you can comfortably take the time to hold your events.

Using Your Calendar Whichever calendar you choose, review it frequently, and especially the last thing Sunday night, or first thing Monday morning. It's important to take a good look at the coming week. While you're at it, you can review how the last week went and move forward anything you didn't get done. This is also an excellent time to look at your goals, and check whether you are still on track.

It's also good to do a mini-review each morning and evening. Note your accomplishments and take a few minutes to consider how the day is going to shape up. Examine your weekly or month-at-a-glance calendar, and your daily to-do list. At the end of the day, think over your accomplishments, reward your work, and fall asleep after reviewing your plans and dreams for the future.

For watercolorist Pam Glasscock, taking this mental time-out is important. "It really helps to take time the night before to think out what I'm going to try to accomplish the next day. This looking ahead has become a mental routine for me. When I don't do this, it always takes me longer to get started in the morning."

Computer and training consultant Bill Dale agrees, but he likes to work with a bigger chunk of time. "I plan the next week every weekend, usually Sunday morning. I also use quarterly planning meetings to review my goals for the next year, and I review these with my accountant about every six months. A wall calendar would be useless to me because I travel so much. I use a planning diary. The key in all time management is to avoid having to copy from one place to another. So I write commitments (in pencil) straight into my diary."

Mid-Range Planning

Mid-range planning involves a time span of six months to two years. The primary planning tool for this period is the cash flow projection, which is described in chapter 3, Financial Strategies. This kind of projection is ideal for time management. When you begin to see the pattern of work and money flowing into and out of your business, you can plan how to spend your time in the future. A cash flow projection is laid out very much like an income statement, but the numbers you plug in are your best guesses about the income you expect or would like to make, and your calculations of the expenses required to keep the business open and to generate that income.

All one-person businesses should use a cash flow projection as a time management tool. With it you will spot problems before they might otherwise have gotten your attention, and you will see how you are doing over time and whether you need to change your behavior in the future. You will also apply the knowledge you gain about such factors as seasonality, which would not be apparent to you if you viewed your business only in a shorter time frame.

Additional mid-range planning tools include wall charts that show major holidays, special events, or commitments you have made that are further in the future than your short-range calendar cover.

Long-Range Planning

Long-range plans are not meant to be set in concrete. They are primarily a framework for goals and desires. When you get lost in the day-to-day operation of the business, they remind you of the reasons you went into business in the first place. As you grow and gain more experience, your long-range vision will probably change, and that is fine. You will find it easier to run a successful business if you make regular appointments with yourself, to go over long-range plans and update them to match who you are becoming and where you want to go. As we said in chapter 4, Information Management, actively cultivating long-range plans and dreams creates a "big picture" context, and a higher level of motivation to do the day-to-day tasks necessary for your long-term success as a businessperson.

Writing down your goals is an important part of successful long-range planning. If you write your goals down and do nothing else except review them in a year or two or even five, you will be surprised at how many of them you have accomplished.

Dress designer Kate Bishop confirms this approach. "About every six months I write down my short-term goals. I put them in front of my appointment book, alongside my long-term goals. I look at them every once in a while. When my short-term goals are accomplished, I make new ones. When I write down my goals, they always get accomplished. It's helpful to see how accomplishing my short-term goals furthers my long-range plans."

In her book, *Wishcraft*, Barbara Sher developed an excellent way to help realize your long-term goals. She recommends creating a "planning wall" upon which to put pictures of your heroes and charts of your plans. These charts include (1) a flow chart, which serves as the master plan to coordinate everything else, (2) a "Tomorrow" section with drawings or pictures representing your long-range goals and a target date for their completion, and (3) a "Next Five Years" section for completion of specific, very concrete goals. You then coordinate this wall chart with a calendar system so that you can break your long-term goals into steps that can be accomplished day to day.

Another idea for keeping your long-range goals accessible and fresh in your mind is to put them in a notebook you keep next to your bed so that you can review them just before falling asleep.

OFFICE HOURS

To manage your time effectively, you will need to exercise control over people who just happen by, as well as those who come for an appointment or during store hours. A one-person business has its own tempo and rhythm. Setting hours is easy for some businesses and hard for others. The best way to maintain control over your business time is to set hours of operation and make sure everyone knows what they are. Many small businesses have office or store hours on Monday through Friday, from 9:00 A.M. to 5:00 P.M. Clearly, they are encouraging people to call and come by during these hours, and people will. To allow time to attend to anything which takes you away from the office, or for uninterrupted time to get work done that requires concentration, you may find it necessary to set shorter hours such as 12:00 to 5:00 or by appointment only, etc. As a one-person business, you cannot simply shut your door and tell your secretary to hold all calls, so it's crucial that you make some workable policy and stick to it.

Before any visitor ever reaches your business—whether client, customer, friend, or relative—you should make clear what your expectations are about times it is okay to drop by or call your business. Your outgoing phone message and your business cards can contain this information. Inevitably, though, you will still get occasional surprise visitors who drop by at other times. The best way to handle a surprise visitor is to decide immediately whether you welcome the interruption. Sometimes you might be ready to take a break anyway. If you do not want to visit with them, the best way to handle the situation is by quickly making it known that you are in the middle of some work that requires your full attention and that you cannot stop at the moment. Ask the visitor if they might be available when you are planning to take a break, or during normal business hours, etc.

If you can handle the surprise visits quickly and inoffensively, you will display a professional attitude and will be able to give higher-quality attention to the visitor at a better time.

MEETINGS

In most one-person businesses, meetings consume a lot of time, so it is important to make them as effective as possible. Both one-on-one meetings and group meetings can be set up in ways that make them run more efficiently, take less time, and produce the decisions you need.

One on One

Most of your meetings will probably be with just one other person. You will meet with a customer, a supplier, or someone with whom you are doing a joint project. These meetings will take place on the phone, in your business location, or at your customer's or supplier's place.

Regardless of location, if you take a few minutes before the meeting to prepare, you will profit greatly from it. Make a few notes about the topics you want to cover, the order in which you want to cover them, how long you expect to take, and what you would like the outcomes to be. This kind of preparation will keep the meeting or phone call from deteriorating into a bull session, or ending without your having covered all the reasons the meeting was called in the first place. Then, at the beginning of the meeting, let the other person know what you would like to talk about, how long it might take, and what you would like to see come out of the meeting. Once you have gotten his or her agreement, you can proceed on a much surer footing, entirely unlike the random discussions that so many meetings seem to consist of. This procedure should yield more results arrived at in a more direct fashion. Don't forget, however, to provide for a little time in the beginning and at the end of the meeting for personal exchanges. This will help maintain friendly relations in addition to getting business done.

Group Meetings

Exactly the same procedure can be followed for a meeting attended by three or more people. Many people run meetings according to the old authoritarian model of *Robert's Rules of Order,* if they impose any kind of structure at all. A more effective approach was introduced to the business world in 1985 by Michael Doyle and David Straus in *How to Make Meetings Work.* They describe the various roles that participants can play and the processes that can be used to keep meetings short but have them result in action outcomes. The basic elements are the same as for one-on-one meetings. The difference is that all members of the group are encouraged to make the advance preparation of a list of the topics to cover, the order in which to cover them, the time it should take, and the expected outcomes. Then when the meeting is convened, the group agrees on one person to be the facilitator and one person to be the recorder.

The facilitator starts the meeting by helping to build an agenda out of the topics, priorities, and time limits the participants agree on. During the meeting, the facilitator makes sure that everyone gets a chance to speak, the topics get covered, and the time agreements are kept. The recorder uses a flip chart of large pieces of paper on the wall to record what people are saying throughout the meeting, starting with the selection of the agenda.

These roles are only superficially like the old roles of chairperson and secretary. Unlike the chairperson, the facilitator is not "in charge" of the meeting. In fact, it is recommended that the facilitator not participate in the meeting. In this way he or she can be regarded by the group as being focused on the process of the meeting, while participants focus on the content. The facilitator makes a verbal contract with the group to accomplish this job:

1. I won't contribute my own ideas.
2. I will try to remain neutral.
3. I will focus the group energy on the agenda.
4. I will defend group members from personal attack.
5. I will be the meeting "chauffeur."
6. I will make process suggestions, but basically, "It's your meeting. You decide."

The recorder attempts to build a "group memory" that is a reflection of the consensus of the group rather than the recorder's interpretation of what was said. The recorder does this by using the large paper on the wall and following these seven simple rules:

1. Be brief.
2. Use alternating colored pens.
3. Catch the phrase (noun, verb, object), not the whole sentence.
4. Use bullets to set off key points.
5. Use big margins so the notes are easy to read and points can be added later.
6. Number the pages.
7. Keep checking in with the group to confirm that what was said was correctly recorded.

In rare instances the facilitator or recorder might participate briefly in the meeting, but only if they explicitly and clearly step out of their roles. "Joe, will you take the facilitation for a moment? I think I have something important to say on this topic." "Sally, could you take over the Magic Markers for a minute? I want to say a few words about what Mike just brought up." This option should be exercised only rarely, and only if the group has agreed ahead of time that it is acceptable. So that no on feels left out, the group should pick different people to be facilitator or recorder each time.

We have encountered some interesting group dynamics related to the number of people in a group. When there are fewer than six people, you seldom need a facilitator. In a group this size, something happens to lead all the participants to act as facilitators, making sure that everyone is heard from, no one is attacked, and that the agenda is followed. But the moment you add a seventh person, a facilitator becomes essential. With twelve or more people in a group, it sometimes helps to break up into two smaller groups from time to time, in order to work on a particular agenda item. The two groups might go off into different rooms, or different corners of the same room, for ten or fifteen minutes. After they arrive at a consensus using the facilitative group process, they come back and report to the larger group. The meeting of the whole twelve can then proceed. This approach works remarkably well to move things along when issues arise that the whole group doesn't seem able to resolve.

Tools for Group-Process Decision Making

BEFORE MEETING
- Choose facilitator.
- Gather agenda items.
- Delegate responsibility for each item.
- Divide items into reports/decisions/announcements.
- Bring material and supplies needed.

AT MEETING
- Connect/check-in/share excitement.
- Review agenda items:
    - Prioritize.
    - Set times.
- Contract for roles:
    - Facilitator.
    - Recorder.
- Go through agenda:
    - Take an easy item first (for example, reports before decisions).
    - Break large issues into small parts for discussion.
- Take breaks if meeting is long.
- Make announcements.
- Set next meeting time.
- Evaluate this meeting.
- Close.

RESOURCES

Michael Doyle and David Straus, *How to Make Meetings Work* (New York: Berkeley Publishing Group, 1985).

Alan Lakein, *How to Get Control of Your Time and Your Life* (New York: The New American Library, 1973).

Barbara Sher with Anne Gottleib, *Wishcraft: How to Get What You Really Want* (New York: Ballantine Books, 1979).

James R. Sherman, *Stop Procrastinating—Do it!* (Golden Valley, Minnesota: Pathway Books, 1981).

Two good sources for time management books and supplies are

Day Timers, Inc.
DAY TIMERS, INC.
One Day Timer Plaza
Allentown, PA 18195-1551
215-395-5884

Day Runner
Harper House
3562 Eastham Drive
Culver City, CA 90232
213-837-6900

6

Setting Up Shop

If you are just starting your own business, or if you are moving to a new or bigger location, you have a million little details to work out. All businesses need headquarters, but for a one-person business, having the best possible office environment is critical. Your workplace must be conducive to getting the job done efficiently and, depending on your type of business, it must be pleasant enough to spend a lot of time in and neat enough for clients to visit. Different businesses need different accommodations, so in this chapter we will talk generally about concerns that people have in opening an office and about ways that we and other one-person business owners have responded to them.

THE CHOICE—TO WORK AT HOME OR AWAY FROM HOME

At some point you may face the question of whether to have your business in your home or find a suitable location away from home. There are several common reasons for working from home: You save the expense of an outside location. You have a short commute. You can get up from bed in the middle of the night, or walk from the living room to your office, whenever you have a good idea or just an urge to work.

The arguments against working from home include local zoning restrictions that prohibit it and weak psychological boundaries. That same convenience of being able to work whenever you want to can also lead to the sense that you are always at work, that you can't seem to get away from it. To combat this feeling, you might reorganize your work space so that the aesthetic boundaries reinforce stronger psychological boundaries. Sue, a travel agent, visits her wealthy clients at their home or office to assist them in planning for their "adventure" vacation. Back at home, Sue has created an office environment that sets the stage for total concentration. Once inside her office she draws the curtains, turns on the lights, closes the door, and settles down to work. When she is finished for the day she reverses the process and leaves her work behind. If you cannot actually close the door to your work space, perhaps you can create a screen of some sort, or if necessary move your office out of your home.

Working in a regular business location can often give you an image of professionalism that is just not possible from your home, no matter how nice it is. Also some clients or customers expect you to be in an outside location and are hesitant to do business with someone who works out of the home. Maintaining an outside office is almost always more costly than running your business from home, and it is sometimes not as convenient. But offsetting these disadvantages are clearer boundaries and a more professional image.

OFFICE AT HOME, WITH FAMILY— SPECIAL CONSIDERATIONS

I wanted to spend more time with my family.
I didn't want to miss watching my kids grow up.
Just once I wish I could be the one who bakes the brownies and helps with the school play.

We often hear statements such as these, and in fact, being home and available to children is one of the leading reasons for the rapid growth of one-person businesses. In addition to wanting to be there for their children, many people are aware that running their business from home allows their children to develop the attributes of tradeskill we discussed in chapter 1. By living with a business, children absorb a sense of what business is about and why it can be rewarding. They will have more options when the time comes to choose between seeking employment and creating a business of their own.

Being your own boss and working from home gives you flexibility. You can make the time to attend an important track meet at school, or just to get to know your children's friends. And with the time that would otherwise go to commuting and dealing with office politics, you can also become more active in your community. All of this sounds, and is, wonderful, but it doesn't happen magically.

To make it work requires planning on your part, especially as regards spillover and child care.

Spillover

"Spillover" occurs when your small child races to answer the door for a client, or picks up the phone to answer an important overseas call. Spillover is having the dog answer the door. It is two cats racing around your office during an intense moment in a therapy session. It is your husband politely knocking to inquire whether you want to go next door for dinner tonight. In general, spillover is having your personal or home life intrude upon your work—a major nuisance that requires a lot of thought and some experience to avoid. Solving this problem is tricky because in creating a family, the whole idea is to be open and available to each other. But an office in the home makes it necessary to create some boundaries.

Eliminating spillover involves four main considerations: reducing noise, avoiding interruptions, providing adequate child care, and maintaining good communication with family members, particularly children. If clients come to your home, you must make your space fit their expectations of professionalism. They must feel that you are offering them the best of service, including your undivided attention. Homelike noises always seem intrusive in a professional setting, so do whatever is necessary to keep your office separate from family affairs. You may need to set up shop in an outside building or in the basement or attic, or actually soundproof your office space.

It is also essential to establish your uninterrupted working hours with your family and together to develop rules dealing with clients coming to your home. To avoid interruptions, try to have a door that you can close, which family members are permitted to open only in an emergency. The idea of an emergency varies from person to person, and to a child, losing a ball could be considered an emergency. Make certain everyone clearly understands what is meant by emergency.

Child Care

Child care is perhaps the most difficult issue to deal with. After all, if you chose to work at home in order to be near your children, what have you accomplished if you send them away to be taken care of? Our rule is this: If your children are in school full time, then you can work around their schedule, hire someone to come in for the few hours after school, involve them in part of your work, etc. If they are not in school for a full day, then you will have to hire someone to look after them. This probably means sending them away from home—unless you have a huge house with a live-in unflappable grandparent who enjoys spending their entire day with the grandchildren. To attempt to make very young children conform to your business requirements can be downright cruel; it is also probably impossible.

Communication is crucial, and especially so if having a business in the home is new for your family. Suddenly the rules are different. Rooms are off-limits. You are home but not home. A child with something to share has to wait until a certain time. In the excellent book, *Working From Home*, Paul and Sarah Edwards cover in-depth all of these issues and much more. Regarding communicating with your children, they emphasize giving them as much information as possible about when and where you will be working, when you will and won't be available, who will be available when you can't be, and exactly what is expected from them. As the Edwards explain in their book:

> Some questions children may be troubled with in connection with your working at home include:
>
> Am I still important?
> How much can I get away with?
> Are you still available to me when I need you?
> Who is going to be in charge?

When you work from home, you must provide your own structure and make up your own rules about space, privacy, and accessibility, all of which is challenging at first. With perseverance and a lot of support from your family, however, you may wonder how you ever did it any other way. Business advisor Paul Terry, who seems to have an ideal office-home arrangement, smiles with satisfaction when he explains how he managed to make it work so well. "I've found lately that I am much more effective in my business. I no longer work on weekends, for instance, and I have a much higher income than I did a couple of years ago. Two years ago my children's schedules were very disruptive. They went to two different schools and had different hours and I was involved in carpooling and being available to them when they came home. Now they attend the same school, and both leave at 7:30 in the morning, and they return at 2:30 in the afternoon. We have a housekeeper who takes care of them until 5:30. This is an ideal arrangement for everyone, and it's made all the difference to me. I can get an early start, which allows me to take a two-hour lunch with a friend or colleague and still put in an eight-hour day and have the weekends free to be with my family."

OFFICE LAYOUT

A useful metaphor for the best possible working environment for a one-person business is the cockpit of an airplane. All the controls necessary to get the vehicle off the ground, fly from point to point, and land safely are within easy reach. The dials and meters that give us ongoing readouts on how fast we are moving, how high we are, whether the plane is level, climbing or falling, if there are other planes in the vicinity and if we are headed for a collision with them, and so forth, are also easily read from the pilot's seat. The pilot never has to leave that seat and go to some other part of the aircraft to move a control or read a gauge.

The same compactness should be true of your actual working environment. Both the physical plant (your office or store) and your information environment (your books, mailing lists, filing systems, etc.) can be organized with efficiency in mind.

"Most everything I need is within three feet of me, so I can access data very quickly," explains Paul Terry. "The files on current clients are in the left-hand drawer of my desk, and the phone log is kept on top of the desk. When a new client calls in I pull out a blank inquiry form and get the basic information I need in order to work with them. Then I send out whatever they need along with a note. I keep a memo of what I have sent them in an inquiry file that I keep on my desk. If they become a client, I open up a file folder for them, with the basic information on the first page. Any subsequent meetings are also filed there. As long as a client is current, their file stays in the file drawer in my desk. If they become noncurrent, they go into a nearby file cabinet."

Suzanne Maxson, job development researcher, has two basic work areas. "I have a table where I keep intake forms. When I get a referral I put the filled out forms there. This is work I need to look at and organize. The other table is where I've got my printed forms and notes about phone calls I have to make and reports I have to write. Every time I walk into the office I look at both tables and can see what I need to do. I can easily see if things are piling up over here and nearly cleared out over there. If there's a pile I know I have to work late that day. Everything is right there close at hand."

Photographer Norman Prince uses a color-coded filing system. "I keep one file for each company, each individual, or each division of each company. These are right next to my typewriter. My green files are for projects that are going smoothly; the yellow ones are for projects that need special attention. In the closet, in red files, are the projects I don't need to have access to as much, the ones that are either historical or void. Then I have two milk crates with hanging files full of potential client information. I keep them near the desk, but not in immediate reach."

RULES FOR ORGANIZING YOUR WORK SPACE

Several basic principles can be applied to the physical organization of your work space.

1. Make it easy to tell where to replace an object or tool after you have moved it. For tools, a good method is to hang a pegboard on the wall, figure out where each tool should be hung for maximum efficiency, and then draw an outline around the tool when it is in place. If the pegboard

is dark, draw a white or light-colored outline; if it is light, draw a black or dark outline. Then whenever you take down several tools at a time, it will be easy to hang them back up where they are supposed to go. Your original decision about where they should go will be maintained.

2. Keep the most frequently used objects, tools, and supplies closest at hand. This rule takes precedence over logical structures such as alphabetizing. The opposite of this rule applies to storage of old documents and seldom used tools.

3. Avoid built-in desks or other fixtures. Use adjustable shelving. Buy a pair of two-drawer file cabinets rather than a four-drawer unit. You can put a board across the pair to make a desk, or you can stack them, like a four-drawer cabinet, to take up less floor space. A modular approach allows you to change your office arrangement when your needs or aesthetics change. Lightness and flexibility are desirable because you are always learning how to be more efficient. Avoid furniture or equipment difficult to change or adjust.

4. Never put something heavy above you where it could fall and injure you. Heavy objects should be lifted up, not down, so store them underneath or below other fixtures, or in the bottom of shelves or cabinets.

5. It is easier to look down than up. Most desks stand twenty-four to twenty-nine inches high, so that when you sit in a normal chair, you naturally look down at the desktop and at any work or equipment on it. If you are using a computer, always position it so that the center of your monitor is about seventeen inches in front and about six inches lower than your eye level, or square with your chin, when you are sitting in your normal work chair. One caution, however: Looking down for long periods of time places a strain on the natural curve of your neck that can lead to such symptoms as neck aches and headaches. To prevent this, you should take regular breaks to stretch and relax your neck. You can also help your neck by sitting up straight, back supported, with ears aligned with your shoulders and your chin tucked slightly under.

6. When using a telephone, try to find a way to keep your hands free. There are good telephone headsets on the market, but don't get the kind that stick the headphone speaker into the channel of your ear. This can cause trouble with wax buildup. Also watch out for the cheap Asian imitations. We have had the best experience with Plantronics brand headsets. They are more expensive than most, running in the $50 to $90 range, but they are much more reliable and comfortable, as well as having much better speaker quality and mouthpiece microphones.

7. Be health conscious. Avoid the coffee-to-get-up, alcohol-to-come-down syndrome. Good health requires that you stand up and move often. Sitting for long hours isn't good for your body. Good chairs and posture are important, as are fresh air, visual diversion, and control of noise level.

FURNITURE AND FIXTURES

Because a one-person business must be very efficient and cost conscious, we have gathered together a sizable amount of information about what works the best to promote health and provide a maximum of efficiency at a minimum of cost. So in addition to the general principles of office layout, here are some specific points to be aware of when choosing the furniture and fixtures that will go into your working environment. The major areas of concern are lights, chairs, storage systems, and desks or other working surfaces.

Lights

With lights, placement and quality are the main concerns. Place your light sources so that light comes from behind your head whenever possible. For close-up work, however, which requires direct lighting of the work surface, such as pasteup of a newsletter, you would need either two separate lights, or a light that can be adjusted. Many lighting systems are easily adjustable. The most widely known is the swing-arm lamp, available in most hardware, office supply, and furniture stores, which has two spring-loaded arms that allow you to move the light toward or away from the work surface, and in a 360-degree arc. This makes it possible to point the light almost anywhere you need it. Also, lamps like this can be easily moved. The lighting in Claude's home and office consists almost entirely of swing-arm lamps, which work equally well in the kitchen, living room, bedroom, or office. He has purchased several different kinds of mounting brackets, including a couple of floor stands, some lead-weighted desk stands, and the normal screw brackets that allow these lamps to be mounted to a desktop or wall. Luxo is the most well-known brand of swing-arm lamps, but there are less expensive brands of equal quality.

Quality of light, the other major lighting concern, involves choosing between natural, incandescent, or fluorescent light. Many people feel that indirect natural light is the best. Some people just like the looks of it, and others think it is healthier. Ultraviolet light, or UV, is the source of Vitamin D from the sun. Getting forty-five minutes or more of outdoor light each day is essential for maintaining normal health, and it is the UV part of the light that is most important. However, even if your workplace has windows or skylights, and you can control the light coming in with shutters or shades, most of the ultraviolet light is screened out by the glass or plastic, if not by the shutters or shades.

You can replace some of the needed daylight with a type of fluorescent lighting known as full spectrum. In addition to providing some missing UV, this light allows you to see things in their true colors, instead of in the yellowish color of incandescent lighting, the blue of "cool" fluorescents, or the reddish yellow of "warm" fluorescents. Studies conducted for over a decade have indicated that people who work under full spectrum lights experience improvement in visual acuity, more energy, and fewer colds or illnesses than people who don't. The best-known brand of full spectrum tubes is manufactured by DuraTest and sold under the brand name Vita-Lite.

The only drawback to full spectrum lighting is expense. The light tubes themselves are two to four times more expensive than regular fluorescent tubes. But if you take into account that they are five to ten percent less expensive to operate than the equivalent incandescent lights, you may be able to justify the investment. If not, then you will have to choose between incandescent and regular fluorescent.

Fluorescent lights provoke a lot of debate, with the number of vocal critics on the rise. The electricity coming into our homes and offices oscillates at the rate of sixty times per second. This is a function of how it is manufactured, and we need not understand the technicalities of this process in order to discuss the problem it causes. Many people who work under fluorescent lights have seen them flicker, either subliminally or out of the corner of their eyes, and it makes them uncomfortable, tense, irritable, or worse. Although it is true that fluorescent lights do flicker, research has shown that usually less than ten percent of the population will notice it if the power modulators or ballasts used to run fluorescent lights are in good condition. All too often, however, the ballasts are ignored until the lights are flickering so badly that everyone can see it, or they start to hum so loudly that no one can miss it. This ballast problem affects full spectrum tubes also. The solution is to maintain your lights by changing the ballasts when they start to wear out.

Regardless of whether you choose incandescent or fluorescent lighting, make certain you spend an hour or more outdoors each day to get your daily dose of Vitamin D. You cannot completely replace your need for natural sunlight with full spectrum lighting. But if you are going to use fluorescent fixtures, it is a good idea to replace all the tubes with full spectrum tubes as a supplement. Those of you who want full spectrum lighting, but already have incandescent fixtures should look for incandescent full spectrum lights known as daylight bulbs. There is also a new kind of incandescent light manufactured in Canada that uses a compound known as neodimoxide to coat the inside of the bulb. This compound absorbs yellow light, so that the light from these bulbs approaches full spectrum.

Chairs

As a one-person business manager you may spend twenty to thirty percent of your life sitting in a chair. The human body was not meant to sit for hours at a time, so aside from moving about periodically, you should give your body as much support as possible by sitting in a good chair at the right height. Your chair is the single most important piece of furniture you can buy. It will help prevent the potential ailments and diseases that can arise from the unnatural behavior of sitting.

Many different kinds of chairs are available, but there are just a few simple features to look for. Your chair should encourage you to sit with proper posture. The back of the chair should fit firmly into the lumbar, or lower, region of your back. The chair should be high enough from the floor that when you sit in it, your feet rest flat on the floor. Coordinate the height of your chair with the height of your desk. Sit upright in your chair and let your arms drop relaxed at your side. Then bend your arms at the elbow. Your hands should be resting on the surface of your desk as you hold your lower arms, from the elbow to your hands, straight out from your body. At worst, there should be only a slight upward bend. For most people, this makes the desk surface from twenty-four to twenty-nine inches from the floor. You can always adjust your chair height so that your arms are in the correct position, and then put your feet on a stool or footrest if they do not reach the floor, or buy a chair with a built-in footrest. Chairs that are easily adjustable usually cost more, but they are worth it.

If you have more than one working surface, each a different height from the floor, you may want a chair with hydraulic adjusters. These will allow you to quickly readjust your seat height for whichever work surface you are using. Another important feature is casters. A chair with large, smooth-rolling casters can glide across carpet or bare floors with ease. This can be of particular help if you have an L-shaped desk or a small office with two or more desks close together. With a rolling chair you can move quickly from one working surface to another, and you won't need to take up space with a second chair.

If you are stuck with older non-ergonomic chairs, you can lessen the negative effects of sitting in them for hours at a time by using foam wedges and lumbar cushions. These are more widely available now, even appearing in auto parts stores for use while driving. If you have trouble finding them, ask your doctor or a local chiropractor.

Desks and Working Surfaces

Desktops tend to be loaded down from time to time, and should therefore be able to carry the load. Most decent-quality desk furniture meets this requirement, but be sure to keep it in mind when you are shopping around.

With working surfaces, flexibility means that you can easily move a unit from one place to another, and you can use it for more than one purpose. A $20 door set on two file cabinets is much more flexible than a $500 oak rolltop desk. If decor plays a part in your decision, you will have to be creative. Charmian Anderson, a therapist, created a flexible desk using an oval piece of glass spanning two beautiful brass table stands. The principle is the same as for a door and two file cabinets, but this variation fits better into the decor of her elegant office. It meets her need for flexibility, too, because she can move it easily. And with dimensions of three by six feet, it could serve as a meeting room table if necessary.

Storage Systems

For safe occasional access, cardboard archive boxes are a good choice. If stored in a dry place, cardboard is all you really need. If want to protect some of your records from fire, then you will need a fireproof file cabinet. For fast easy access, filing cabinets are best. But depending on the setup of your work space, you might find such alternatives as Crate-A-File useful. Crate-A-Files are plastic boxes similar to milk crates that can be stacked one on top of another; they include metal or plastic runners for holding letter-sized hanging folders. Both crate-type files and regular filing cabinets are available with casters. This added flexibility allows you to move them easily from one location to another, eliminating the need to cross the room to pull files out and put them back. It also makes a small space seem bigger because you can roll the files out of the way when they are not in use.

What doesn't fit into a filing drawer or box will probably go on a shelf. Most hardware and furniture stores sell modular shelving. It comes in two basic forms: on-the-wall bracket systems and knock-down cubical systems. On-the-wall systems are fully adjustable but require you to put holes in the wall; they are therefore semipermanent. Cubical systems are stackable and simply need to be assembled and put into place; they can serve as moving boxes if you change offices.

Noise Control

Noise is a very important consideration in setting up your workspace. Paul and Sarah Edwards have done a good job explaining why in their book *Working From Home.*

"Noise was the number one environmental concern identified by office workers in the Lou Harris poll for Steelcase, a leading office furniture manufacturer. This is not surprising, because even moderately high noise levels cause increased blood pressure, faster heartbeat, and other symptoms of stress, while excessive noise causes fatigue, distraction, and errors in work.

"While too much noise certainly interferes with work, a total absence of sound is also stressful. As one-person who moved his office home says, 'The first thing I noticed was the silence. I never realized how much I appreciated the sounds of the office.'

"Just how much sound do you need to stay mentally alert? Probably not more than thirty decibels, about the sound of normal air conditioning. Even better would be twenty decibels of sound, about equivalent to leaves rustling in the breeze.

"The average office has a noise level of about fifty decibels. The sound of an average conversation is about sixty decibels, while the vacuum cleaner in your home runs at about eighty decibels. Prolonged exposure to over seventy decibels may result in hearing impairment.

"Here are are several sound control techniques that they recommend:

1. Draperies over windows. For maximum effectiveness, these need to be lined and floor length.
2. Ceiling treatments such as acoustical tile or commercially applied sound-absorbent material.
3. A thick pile carpet with an underpad to absorb noise in the room.
4. Heavily padded furniture.
5. Weather stripping on doors and windows.
6. Indoor barriers such as room dividers or screens; outdoor barriers such as a concrete block wall over five feet high.
7. Solid core doors in place of hollow-core doors.
8. Double glazed windows.
9. Wall coverings such as fabric or cork.
10. Acoustical drywall with thick insulation placed between the studs of the new wall, or paneling on top of your existing walls.

"Before you spend a lot of money or time on any of these sound control measures, however, find out if the noise is coming through a heat or air vent. If it is, using one of the sound 'masking' techniques described below will be more effective.

"To produce enough sound to keep yourself alert when working at home alone, you can create your own background noise. Consider using sounds like these while you work.

1. A stereo playing low.
2. A gurgling fish tank with a water filter and air pump.
3. A cage of songbirds such as canaries.
4. A 'white noise' generator.
5. One of the commercially available records or endless-loop tape cassettes that play sounds from nature such as the sea and the wind.

"Because these sounds are rhythmical, they will also help mask noise you can't screen out by other measures."

RESOURCES

Paul and Sarah Edwards, *Working From Home* (Los Angeles: Jeremy P. Tarcher, 1988).

Home Office Computing, a monthly magazine on the issues of working from home, with emphasis on office equipment, especially computers. 730 Broadway, New York, NY 10003; 212-505-3580.

National Home Business Report, a quarterly now in its sixth year of publication, providing access to other small business networks, individuals, and businesses. National Home Business Network, Box 2137-P, Naperville, IL 60565.

Working Mother, a monthly magazine focusing on the concerns of working mothers, including those who work from home. 230 Park Avenue, New York, NY 10169; 800-525-0643.

7

Choosing Office Equipment— High Tech or Low?

Many machines and devices are available to help you run your one-person business. Two of them, the answering machine and the typewriter, stand out as efficiency boosters. They are essential pieces of office equipment.

This chapter will give you a set of criteria and a selection process for evaluating any office equipment, from answering machines and typewriters, photocopiers and facsimile machines, to cellular phones and computers. We will use photocopiers and computers to demonstrate this selection process, but you can adapt it to help you decide whether to add any additional office technology to your equipment inventory.

EVALUATING TECHNOLOGY—FEATURES VERSUS COST

"He who dies with the most toys wins!" is a popular and seductive notion of the day. But an effectively run one-person business will absolutely avoid this game. If you have plenty of discretionary income and want to take pleasure in playing with the latest electronic and mechanical toys, then have at it. For anyone else, be sure that keeping your toy box full of the newest and neatest can be comfortably justified as a wise business decision.

The best way to avoid high-tech consumeritis is to resist the impulse to buy something just because it is new. Develop an approach, like the one described in this chapter, that you consistently use to help you decide when to buy a new machine and whether it makes economic sense.

The trade-off between features and cost is the first important consideration in deciding whether to purchase office technology. The manufacturers of most office equipment offer their products with a range of features. Sometimes the lower end of this range is perfectly suitable, in both price and capability, for a particular function you would like to perform. Although other criteria can be added to your selection process, the features-versus-cost consideration is a basic one and in many cases will suffice.

Telephone Answering Machines

Of all the equipment you might buy to make running your one-person business easier, the telephone answering machine tops the list. We have given many reasons why this is so in chapter 4, Information Management.

A wide variety of telephone answering machines is on the market, and our clients have reported the best success with Panasonic and Radio Shack models. These two brands seem to be well built and to have more features than many others. Brand name is not the main consideration, however. Shop for features first, and price second. Look for three key features: (1) a voice-activated, unlimited incoming message, (2) remote message retrieval, and (3) the ability to change the outgoing message from a remote phone. Low-end units cost as little as $50 to $75, but lack voice activation, remote access, or some other feature. In the $75 to $100 range you will almost always get these features. Be sure to buy a power-surge protector to go along with your machine, as many of the newer, solid-state models will burn out from sudden brown-outs in your local power system.

Typewriters

At a very basic level, the office machine that comes next in importance after the answering machine is not the computer but the typewriter. For many one-person businesses the computer represents a level of power that is overkill and a level of learning that is overwhelming. In any case, it is best to try out a system manually before you automate it. If you have a manual system that works, you should carefully weigh the costs and benefits of putting it on a computer. You want to avoid the many problems that can arise, which we discuss later in this chapter.

The typewriter makes your one-person business easier to operate in several ways. First, it's easy to use. Second, it's faster than handwriting. Third, it can actually automate many of your simpler writing tasks without the trouble and expense of a computer. Let's evaluate typewriters by comparing features versus cost in some detail.

Features With the new electronic typewriters, even people who type with the hunt-and-peck method can bang out letter-perfect documents, forms, and envelopes. Most of these machines have a small liquid crystal display (LCD) panel above the keyboard that allows you to preview what you are typing and make automatic corrections (from one to three lines of text) before you commit it to paper.

For only a bit more you can buy models that will permit you to store information that you use over and over—for instance, addresses or phrases or paragraphs, such as your closing to a letter. This capability can save you a tremendous amount of time. Some models also have spell checking. At the top end in price and features are typewriters with disk drive and monitors, giving you most of the features of a computer while maintaining the familiarity and ease of use of a typewriter. If letters and short documents constitute the bulk of your written output, a word-processing typewriter might well be the perfect tool.

Costs The new electronic typewriters run from $250 to $1,500. In general, the price of most high-tech office machines is cut in half every two years, until a new generation of features and benefits is introduced. For instance, five years ago an IBM Selectric that used interchangeable font balls and could correct one character at a time would cost $1,200 new. Today, several manufacturers sell models that use interchangeable font daisy wheels and can correct several lines at a time for under $500, and you can buy a clone of the original IBM Selectric for under $300. It is therefore best to temper the need for increased efficiency or output with patience, and to wait until the equipment with the features you want falls into your price range.

By balancing the low cost against the required features, most one-person businesses can easily justify the purchase of a typewriter, at least a basic low-end model.

ON THE LOOKOUT FOR TECHNOLOGY FOR YOUR BUSINESS

Long before you know about a technology, you may be aware of parts of your business that could benefit from automation. By paying attention to your communications needs and the way in which information flows through your business, you will be ready to evaluate any new technology that looks like an economical and effective way to streamline your business.

The central valley of California has seen the growth of a network of professional agricultural consultants. These people specialize in knowing how to control the pests and diseases that infect farm crops. Because their clients are farmers who live very far apart, and because their work requires them to be in the field for most of the day, the consultants needed a special communications system—

one that allowed them to respond to their clients' urgent calls, without going back to the office several times a day.

Answering machines weren't the solution: Since the consultants weren't near telephones, they had no way of retrieving messages from their machines. Instead, they turned to citizens band or shortwave radio with a home-base station. A farmer could contact a consultant's home base by phone or radio, knowing that the consultant's spouse or partner could relay the message by radio. The consultant would then get back to the farmer as quickly as possible, or drop by if the farmer was nearby.

As you might expect, these agricultural consultants were among the first to use cellular phones when broadcast stations were built in their areas. Because they were already aware of their communication needs, they easily recognized a new technology that could make their system run more smoothly. Also, the cost of a cellular phone dropped rapidly from $3,000, when they were introduced in 1984, to less than $1,000 by 1987—making it an affordable technology in a very short time.

This is a perfect example of one-person business owners who were ready to take advantage of a new technology when it came along. They knew what they needed, and quickly recognized the additional flexibility that cellular phones would provide, as well as the difference in service that they would make.

Possibilities like this will occur to you as you become aware of the needs of your business and of existing technologies that are just now reaching an affordable price range. Cellular phones, facsimile machines, photocopiers, and computers are among the low-cost technologies that you may want to look at from this perspective.

QUESTIONS TO ASK ABOUT ANY TECHNOLOGY

Regardless of low cost, you should never buy any technology until you absolutely need it. You can determine this by asking the following questions:
- Will it reduce my expenses?
- Will it increase my income?
- Will it save time or increase my output?

In addition, you will need to evaluate the true costs of buying and using any new technology. Ask these basic questions:
- Is it a very new technology, or has it been around for a while?
- How much will supplies and maintenance cost?
- How long will it take me to learn to use it?
- Will I have to continue to use the old manual system too, until I know for sure that the new technology works?
- What will be the additional costs, such as special furniture or accessories?
- What is the real life of the equipment?

With these questions as guidelines let's look at photocopiers and computers. You could use this same process to evaluate any high technology purchase.

Photocopiers

Will it reduce my expenses? Making photocopies usually costs between 5 and 10 cents a copy if you do your copying at a commercial location. With your own copier you can bring the cost down to from 2 to 6 cents a copy. However, when you own a copier you will probably make at least half again as many copies as you did before, because it is so convenient.

Will it increase my income? This is hard to measure, since usually you will not be selling the photocopies themselves. But then you can quickly and easily copy an article or letter and send it to a client or customer, thus expanding your communications and opening up a different kind of relationship, the result may be increases in business.

Will it save time or increase my output? You will definitely save time when you have your own copier, even if you make more copies than you used to. Organizing the material to be copied and then going out to a photocopy store is always more time-consuming.

Is this a new technology, or has it been around awhile? Photocopiers have been around long enough that it is difficult to find a bad one. Although certain models or brand names are better than others, they all operate at a more or less common level of performance. This makes it necessary to look to additional features, rather than performance, as the criteria for choosing one.

How much will supplies and maintenance cost? This is the trickiest question for photocopiers because toner cartridges and drums vary greatly in cost. It is important to find out how many copies you get per toner cartridge. If you buy a model that has a separate toner cartridge and drum, you need to know the average life expectancy of the drum. Figured over the time you expect to be using the machine, expensive toner and short-lived drums can make an inexpensive copier cost more than an expensive model that is more economical to operate.

Copiers are usually low-maintenance machines. To keep them trouble free have them serviced once a year. You can buy a service contract for a few hundred dollars, or you can pay $50 to $100 per hour each time you call the service technician out. Ask others who have copy machines about the service record on their machines, or check recent reviews in magazines like *Consumer Reports*.

How long will it take me to learn to use it? For photocopiers, this is not a very important question. They are all easy to use, and it usually takes only a few minutes to learn. It's when something goes wrong inside the machine that you might have trouble. All have different instructions for removing jammed paper or replacing the heating element. Ask about fixing these problems before buying, to see if you understand the procedures and whether you could do them yourself in an emergency. You don't want to have to pay for a service call just to remove a piece of jammed paper.

Will I have to continue to use the old manual system too? For longer runs and for collating, folding, or binding services, it is still best to go to an offset printer or photocopy store. You can confirm this by checking prices in your area. But remember to include your time as one of the cost factors.

What about additional costs? Most personal copy machines are small enough that you won't need any special furniture. Still you may want to buy one of the small stands that have space for paper and supply storage built in. You may also want to buy accessories such as paper trays, or automatic collators. Another useful purchase might be a desktop page folder. It will cost around $200 to $300 dollars and can fold up to three sheets at a time of regular 8-1/2-by-11-inch paper to fit into a number 10 envelope. If you make a lot of photocopies that you mail, one of these machines will pay for itself with saved time in the first year you have it.

What is the real life of the equipment? This is an important question because it's too easy to equate equipment life with the depreciation schedule that is set up for tax deduction purposes. Most equipment lasts significantly longer than its depreciation life. If you use the true life expectancy of the equipment in your cost calculations, it can change your decision.

So, should I buy a photocopier? That depends. If it will truly save time and money, it will probably be a good investment. Relating it to your level of income might be the safest thing to do once you have decided it would be a good idea. If you make $50,000 a year, and you want to spend only one percent of your income, what kind of a photocopier can you buy for $500? The good news is that you can buy a simple plain-paper copier that will make 8-1/2-by-11-inch copies for under $500. The bad news is that you usually have to load the blank paper one sheet at a time, and there are virtually no features, such as different page size or enlargement and reduction.

More good news is that you will find the rest of the personal copiers range in price from $700 to $1,700. These machines produce about six to ten copies a minute and are a good choice if you need fewer than a thousand copies a month. Moreover, copy quality is just as good as the most expensive business copiers.

Computers

A computer is better than anything else at sorting numbers and letters at super-fast speeds. This capability may help you do things faster than normal, but it also allows you to make mistakes faster than normal. And you can expend a lot of energy and lose a lot of sleep trying to get a computer to do what you want. For these reasons alone deciding to buy a computer is not as simple as choosing a typewriter or a photocopier. Because a computer can do many different things, and also get you into trouble very easily, you have to ask yourself a few extra questions. You have to (1) decide what you want it to do, (2) find the software that does that, and (3) buy the hardware that particular software runs on.

Decide what you want the computer to do. This is a bit more difficult than it sounds. There are many software packages available today to take advantage of what a computer can do, but only a few of them will be of real use to a one-person business. Computer salespeople will tell you that you can completely change your life by getting a computer. Then they will proceed to sell you the hardware with little consideration for what you need done. Or they will tell you that all you need is word processing, database, and spreadsheet or accounting software. Seldom do they take the time to get to know you and your business and to discover what your unique needs might be.

The computer is a fun toy, and tasks it can do to help a business include accounting, list management, sales tracking, inventory, desktop publishing, letter writing, graphic presentations, financial analysis, and many more. But when you decide to computerize you should do it a small bit at a time. So make a list of all the things you want the computer to do for you, and prioritize it. Start by shopping for a solution for the most important function. Don't try to find a computer that will do everything you need right from the start. Computer technology changes rapidly, but computerizing your business should proceed slowly and carefully. By the time you are ready to computerize some of your lower priority tasks, you may be able to afford an even better system, or one better suited for doing that particular task. For example, if your primary need is for desktop publishing, there is no doubt that the best solution is software written for the Apple Macintosh. But if fast word processing and spreadsheet analysis is more important to you, an IBM or IBM compatible is not only better, but much faster.

Find the software that does what you want. Unless you are a computer programmer, want to get deeply involved in modifying the software, or are willing to hire someone to help, you should concentrate on the three types of software that will come ready to use without a lot of practice or modifications: telecommunications software, word processing software, and list management software.

Telecommunications Software Most one-person businesses will find using a modem (a device that allows your computer to talk to another computer over the phone) to be fun, but only marginally useful, so telecommunications may not be high on your list. But if your business sells information, you might find one of the many databases and commercial conferencing systems to be of value, and they are accessible over the phone, using a modem. If you are isolated by geography or circumstances, you can find emotional and technical support on local, regional, and national conferencing systems. If you are a writer, you may want to exchange computer document files with your coauthors or send your finished manuscripts to your editor over the phone. But for other than information-oriented businesses, telecommunications will have marginal value.

Word Processing Software The advantages of word processing are best experienced by a business that creates a lot of reports, letters, or other documents. If your business requires only a few letters or forms, you will probably be better off using a typewriter. Word processing allows you to create a document much faster than you can with a typewriter. You can type much faster with word processing software, forgetting about spelling, punctuation, grammar, or what the document will look like when it is printed. Afterward you can go back and make all the corrections and modifications you like before you print. This takes much less time than the old way of composing several drafts on your typewriter before you got one just right. With word processing you can make corrections and reformat a document as many times as you like before committing it to paper.

Once you master this way of "processing words," however, you'll find that, as with a photocopier, you start creating many more documents or letters than you used to. So the saved time is partially lost to increased output. This is probably to your advantage in the long run. Just as sending out photocopies to clients or associates can be beneficial, using word processing to communicate more frequently can have a subtle positive effect on your volume of business.

List Management Software   Computerized list management shines in cases where you are doing a lot of mailing to clients, customers, or prospects, and you have more than a hundred, but less than a thousand names on your list. It shines because you can use it to sort the names at high speed using whatever criteria you select, alphabetical, by zip code or city, or by any of a number of codes that you may have assigned to each name as you entered it. You can print out labels or envelopes much more quickly than you could type them one at a time. You can create "repetitive personalized letters," where you send the same letter to more than one person, with the computer inserting each person's name and address in the letter for you.

The range of a hundred to a thousand names comes from our experience with dozens of businesses trying to maintain their own mailing lists. If you have less than one hundred names, it is usually easier to handle them manually, in the way we describe in chapter 4, Information Management. For numbers between one hundred and one thousand the computer allows you to handle your own list management quite effectively. With more than one thousand names, maintaining the list takes enough time and energy that you can justify hiring an outside service to do it.

Other lists you might want to computerize include inventory, books, or audio- and videotapes, and—if you are an information or consulting business— the people and businesses that you can refer others to. Except for inventory, these lists are handled pretty much like mailing lists. Software programs have been specifically designed to handle each one of them. For inventory, the applications tend to be specific to a type of business. Check with peers or trade publications to see what is available for your type of business.

What About Accounting Software?   One-person businesses are unique; each one has special accounting needs. Therefore any accounting package you buy will need to be modified to meet those needs. In some cases the modifications may be simple and few, but in others they can be extensive. Some accounting packages are easy to modify and some are not.

Good accounting software is priced from $50 to $4,000 for complete systems. The difference is in how complete they are, how easy they are to modify, and how extensive the report generators are. There are too many packages on the market for us to be able to evaluate them here. And by the time this book comes to print, any specific information given would probably be out of date. But it would be well to keep a few broad issues in mind when considering accounting software.

First, if your manual accounting system works okay now, and doesn't take a lot of time, forget about computerizing it. With even the simplest package, you'll spend more time setting up the software and learning it than it's worth.

Second, think about automating only a part of your system. Perhaps you need just automatic check writing or checkbook balancing, time and billing or accounts receivable, accounts payable or payroll, or inventory. There are many good software packages on the market that do only one of these and do it well. Even if you decide to automate all of your accounting, do only one feature or subsystem at a time, but try to buy all of the modules from the same company so that they can be more easily integrated with each other.

Third, check with others in your field to see if some enterprising company has created a special accounting package specifically for your type of business. These are called vertical market packages and they are available for a growing number of businesses. Among the professions you are likely to find such packages for are: doctors, lawyers, dentists, chiropractors, and accountants. Other fields for which packages have been developed include retail stores, property management, mail-order fulfillment, direct sales, travel agents, and construction. Check with your peers and your trade organization to see what is being recommended for your particular field.

Buy the hardware it runs on. After you have identified your software, the type of computer you need to buy will be obvious. In the United States the major contenders are the Apple Macintosh and the plethora of IBM compatibles manufactured by IBM and a host of other vendors. Most of the IBM compatible hardware components manufactured today, whether in the United States or overseas, are of the same relative reliability. A computer manufactured in Korea will in all likelihood be of equal quality, and last just as long, as a computer manufactured in Japan, Taiwan, Hong Kong, Europe, Canada, or the United States. Quality is more a function of brand and model than point of origin. Even the big companies such as IBM or Compaq buy the same components manufactured throughout Asia and South America.

This means that the most important hardware feature is not hardware at all, but the service and support that come along with it, especially for the IBM compatibles. When you buy your hardware, you can expect a warranty on parts and labor that is good for from ninety days to one year. After the warranty period, you can purchase a service contract for $300 to $500 a year. This works out to be relatively high, since computers are pretty reliable. When they do need fixing, the hourly fee for service runs from $75 to $100, with most repairs lasting less than two hours. But if you don't want to worry about yours being the exception, the service contract could be your best bet.

The most economical sources of support for your hardware (and your software too) are the computer users' groups or special interest groups (SIGs) located in your area. You will have to sift through a lot of advice before you find the answer that actually works, but the cost is low (just membership dues), and the people who populate these groups represent a broad base of experience and knowledge that you can draw on. Groups exist that focus on almost every brand of computer and software package.

Printers—Letter Quality or Laser? One of the most frequently asked hardware questions is, *Should I get a laser printer?* This question can best be answered the same way as you would if you were choosing an entire computer system. What do you want to print? How do you want it to look? Buy the software that does that. Buy the printer the software was written for.

If you want fast, legible printouts, but you are not concerned with how fancy they look, you will probably want to get a dot matrix printer. If the typewritten or letter-quality look is important to you, you will choose between a daisy wheel letter-quality printer or a laser printer. However, the new dot matrix printers, the 24-pin type, come so close to looking like letter quality that many people are choosing them. With a 24-pin printer you can switch between a high-quality near-typewriter look, and a high-speed dot matrix output, both on the same printer. The bubble jet printer is yet another option. Bubble jet printers are whisper-quiet, generating only a forty-five-decibel noise level, as compared to the seventy-five to eighty-five decibels generated by dot matrix or daisy wheel printers. Bubble jet printers are extremely reliable and have a print quality equal to that of a laser printer. They are ideal for most graphics applications and are much faster with graphics than dot matrix printers. The deciding factors will be your personal aesthetics and your budget.

In early 1988, laser printers offering a resolution of 300 dots per inch and print speeds of from six to fifteen pages per minute cost from $1,400 to $5,000. Higher resolution laser printers cost $12,000 or more. Twenty-four-pin printers offering near-letter-quality output at print speeds from 45 to 160 characters per second cost from $500 to $1,500. Daisy wheel letter-quality printers producing a crisp typewriter look at speeds of from 20 to 80 characters per second cost from $200 to $2,000. Good bubble jet printers offering resolutions of 150 to 300 dots per inch at speeds from 20 to 200 characters per second cost about $1,000. The differences in price are a function of features and brand name. Our best advice is to pay as little as possible for the few features you absolutely need. Then wait two or three years until the prices drop to a point where you can buy additional features at a more affordable price—about the time you may need to buy a new printer anyway.

Evaluating Your Computer Choices With all the foregoing in mind, let's run the computer purchase decision through our selection questions.

Will it reduce my expenses? For a one-person business, the answer is usually No, even though having a computer may enable you to reduce the amount you are spending on subcontractors. You won't lower your overall expenses, because you will now use more paper, printer ribbons, envelopes, floppy diskettes, and miscellaneous supplies related to the computer than you ever thought possible. Contrary to the popular belief, using a computer does not lead to a paperless office. Studies sponsored by the Department of Defense to create the so-called paperless office have been going on for more than five years and still haven't managed to eliminate paper completely. Just the opposite is true: Once you get the hang of word processing, you put out more, not fewer, documents than before. Also, wastage increases because you tend to make more corrections when all you have to do is push a button to print out your document again.

If you want to check whether this holds true for you, just add an expense item labeled "computer" to your chart of accounts, and in it post all of the items you buy for the computer. The first year that Claude started making full use of his computer, his office supplies account jumped from $1,500 to $2,300—an increase of thirty-five percent. He has since added a computer account to help him keep costs under control by tracking them more closely.

Will it increase my income? Maybe. At first a computer may have no measurable effect. But if you implement an accounts receivable program that helps you to stay on top of collecting the money owed to you, your income may go up. Or as you master letter writing, promotional mailings, and so forth on the computer, you may see an increase in income that is directly traceable to your use of word processing and list management software. Also, a mail-order business that installs one of the good mail-order fulfillment packages will see a dramatic increase in sales, traceable to an increase in good customer service.

Will it save time or increase my output? After you have gotten through the initial learning curve and are properly set up, you will be able to take advantage of the computer's strongest points, saving time and increasing output. Realizing these two benefits is mostly a matter of picking the right combination of software and hardware, and setting it up correctly.

Is this a new technology, or has it been around awhile? The computer industry is well known for bringing both hardware and software products to market that have not been fully tested and corrected so that they run error free. For this reason, you should avoid buying the latest and greatest software or hardware. Stick to the three questions listed earlier—What do I want the computer to do? What software does that? What hardware does it run on?—and you should be safe from finding yourself the "beta-test site" for some computer vendor. (When a product is almost ready for the commercial market, its creators get a few companies to volunteer to test it in a real-life situation. This is the beta test. After all the things that can go wrong are found and fixed, the product can be offered for sale. Often, however, vendors in the computer industry move too quickly through this stage, and customers who have actually paid for the product become unwilling beta-test sites.)

How much will supplies and maintenance cost? As we said earlier, supply costs will rise. The most critical supply item in a computer system is printer ribbons. You can buy long-lasting ones, but sometimes the shorter-lasting ones are on sale at a price that works out to be cheaper on a per-character basis. Be diligent in shopping for high quality but low price. Ribbons come in two varieties: multistrike and nylon. Contrary to its name, the multistrike ribbon works by passing each place on the ribbon by the print head only once. This gives a clear, crisp look, but means the ribbon can be used only once. Nylon ribbons work on a different principle. They keep going around and around, getting lighter each time, until you finally decide to replace the old faded one with a new fresh one. The standard pricing of the multistrike ribbons makes them appear cheaper, but they aren't really, unless you buy them on sale for a very low price. Let's use ribbons for the NEC Spinwriter to illustrate this point. In 1988, an NEC multistrike ribbon cost $3 or $4, assuming you shopped around. It would give about 180,000 impressions, or about 50,000 impressions per dollar spent. An NEC-brand nylon ribbon cost $4 or $5, but would give nearly 1,500,000 impressions, better than 300,000 impressions per dollar spent. The ratios consistently follow this pattern, regardless of the computer printer you are evaluating. To give you an idea of how much printing this is, the entire contents of this book took around 500,000 impressions. We used up several ribbons just printing out this book, even though they were the nylon type.

An average box of 3,000 sheets of 8-1/2-by-11-inch paper with tractor-feed edges will run between $15 and $30. If you plan to use your computer a lot, you can expect to go through a box every six to eight weeks. You can make a more precise guess by calculating how many pages of documents, letters, invoices, and other printouts you anticipate making.

As we said earlier, the cost of maintenance should be relatively low because computers are fairly reliable. If, however, you choose to buy a service contract after the warranty expires, your costs will go up by $300 to $500 per year. You will need to think ahead in this way in order to know how much more to allow for supplies. Once you know how long supplies will last and what quantity you expect to use, you can easily calculate the increase. A good rule of thumb is to expect your office supply expense to go up by at least twenty to thirty percent.

How long will it take me to learn to use it? This depends on which applications you are going to try to learn. If you buy a Macintosh and use only MacWrite, you will be happily processing documents within a few days of first turning the machine on. If you buy an IBM and an advanced word processing program such as WordPerfect, you will spend a few hours at a time, daily, for several weeks or months in order to master more than half of the program's features. Each type of application has its own learning curve, or period of time over which you master it. Accounting software has a long learning curve; it sometimes takes up to a full year before you can use all of the essential features of a very good package. MacWrite has a very short learning curve, as short as one day for some people.

To figure out the potential learning curve for the packages you intend to buy, ask the salesperson what the average learning time is and then multiply that by a factor of at least two. You can also ask to "test drive" the package, which means that the vendor will set it up on a computer for you to play with. Press on to another store if they say no. Most stores are more than willing to cooperate, since the computer industry needs all the customers it can get. Probably the best way to estimate learning time is by taking an introductory workshop, if any are offered in your area. In a few hours, usually for under $50, you can learn a lot about how difficult a package may be and whether it will to do what you need.

Will I have to continue to use the old manual system too? You bet. It is essential to continue using your old way of doing things until you are completely sure that the computer system works. For most applications the trial period will last only a matter of months. But for something like accounting, you don't want to discover at the end of a quarter or a year that the package you bought doesn't calculate your taxes accurately, and moreover that you don't have any way of figuring them out manually other than redoing everything by hand.

What will be the additional costs? If you plan to spend a lot of time at your computer, it would be wise to give careful consideration to buying special computer furniture. Units that have a special shelf for the printer as well as adjustable shelves for the keyboard and monitor can make it easier to work long hours. Copyholders, diskette storage boxes, a printer stand, and other such accessories can help you stay organized and comfortable while working at the computer. And as we stressed in the section on furniture and fixtures in chapter 6, always give special attention to your chair.

What is the real life of the equipment? Because computers have very few moving parts, they can last years beyond the figures given on depreciation tables. A computer may still be chugging away ten years after you have fully depreciated it. Before a computer wears out it is likely that you will find some new, better software package that runs on a newer computer, and you will want to move up.

Printers are another matter. By their very nature, they beat themselves up as you use them, so you may find yourself buying a new printer after only three or four years. If you buy a top-of-the-line model from a reputable company, you can expect the unit to last at least twice that long. Laser printers are a different matter again. Because the technology used in a laser printer is basically the same as that used in a photocopier, the life of the photoelectric drum is an issue. You can expect a drum to survive 300,000 to 500,000 impressions between replacements. (For a laser printer, as for a photocopier, an "impression" means one whole page.) The remaining moving parts and solid-state circuitry will last several years. As with the computer, it is more likely that you will buy a new laser printer because the features have been improved or the price has dropped than because it has worn out.

Because computers are so durable, computer users often find themselves with one or more computers that just lie around unused. Both Michael and Claude have at least three old computers each that they lend to friends from time to time. Salli, who is usually unimpressed by technological toys, now has two computers—the result of upgrading to a Macintosh less than a year after buying an Apple II.

You might also decide to buy a new computer system when the price finally drops to a level you can afford. As with most high-tech office equipment, the price of computers is cut in half every two years, until a significant change in the technology comes about. For example, Claude bought a Radio Shack TRS Model 100 lap computer for $900 in 1985. It had its own operating system and could run only a small number of packages written specifically for it. It had a 32,000-character memory, no disk drives, and only a small LCD screen that showed eight rows of forty characters each. In 1988 you could spend $900 and buy an IBM compatible laptop computer that will run thousands of different programs, with

---

WHAT ABOUT FAX?

For several years now facsimile machines (FAX) have been available commercially in the range of $2,000 to $10,000, depending upon the features. Since 1988 a wider availability of low cost units aimed at individuals or small businesses has made FAX something to think about.

If you use the selection criteria outlined in this chapter as a guide in purchasing a facsimile, choosing one that will be right for you should be easy. While FAX is becoming used more in business (even restaurants catering to the downtown lunch trade), it still won't replace a telephone answering machine, or a computer with a modem. That is what a FAX really is: a hybrid of the telephone answering machine and a computer with a modem. You can leave a message on someone's FAX machine or receive one on yours, at a time convenient to either of you. And the message you send can be many pages long, with pictures or graphics.

Here are the basic features to look for if you do to decide to buy a FAX: 16-shade gray scale, polling, document autofeed, paper cutter, CCITT Group 3 compatibility, and ease of operations. There are many other features, but these are the ones that are the most important. A machine with all of the basics should run $1,200 to $1,500. Don't be seduced by the apparent glamour of FAX. Think only about whether you have a real need.

A good rule of thumb is that if you FAX 10 to 15 pages a month, you might consider your own machine. As soon as you have your own machine, you will tend to FAX at least twice as much. In 1989 most copy shops charged $3 to $5 a page to send FAX documents for you. The arithmetic shows that replacing a $60/month FAX bill with a lease or purchase payment can make sense, especially if the FAX machine helps your business run more smoothly.

When to forget about FAX? If you never think about it, if nobody asks you for your FAX number, if it just doesn't fit in with the way you run your business, then forget FAX for now.

Guidelines for Buying a Computer

1. A checklist for deciding: Do I want a computer?

( ) I like gadgets.
( ) I read a lot.
( ) I like to spend hours on simple routines like balancing my checkbook.
( ) I like to watch TV.
( ) I like video games.
( ) I like to tinker with appliances and machines.

If you checked three or more, you're probably the type of person that wants a computer, whether you need one or not.

2. A checklist for deciding: Do I really need a computer?

( ) I do financial analyses that require many calculations and recalculations.
( ) I write a lot or am planning to write a book.
( ) I manage a one-person business and need to know what's happening more often than the once a month that I get a report from my accountant.
( ) I am a consultant to middle- or upper-level managers in corporations and make a lot of my recommendations based on information in reports generated by the company's main computer.
( ) I am involved in a computer business.

Any one of these is reason enough to buy a computer. With the price of computer systems dropping each year, it becomes easier and easier to justify buying a computer. There are many good software packages available to help you with each of these functions. If you are a professional or in the specialized retail trades, you can probably find a package designed especially for your business, though you may have to make a thorough search for it.

3. Rules to shop for a computer by.

Memorize these two sets of rules before you go out looking for a computer system.

How to buy a computer:

- Decide what you want it to do.
- Find the software that does that.
- Buy the hardware it runs on.

How to "test drive" the software/hardware system:

Go into as many computer stores as you have the patience to endure. For any software you are interested in ask the salesperson the following:

- Does it do what I want?
- Show me.
- Now let me do it!

The first set of rules will make it difficult for you to purchase a system that fails to do what you need. It will also restrain you from buying more than is necessary.

The second set of rules will help you defend yourself against aggressive, commission-conscious salespeople. A slick salesclerk can demonstrate a package so that it appears to do what you want, but when you get it home, you may have a hard time figuring out how to get it to work again.

a 256,000-character memory, a built-in disk drive storing 800,000 characters on hard-cased floppies, and a large LCD screen that displays twenty-four lines of eighty characters each. Or an IBM compatible desktop computer with a 640,000-character memory, twenty-million-character hard disk and monochrome monitor. In 1987 the NEC Multispeed laptop, with a 640,000-character memory, two 800,000-character disk drives, and a back-lit eighty-character by twenty-four-line screen cost $2,000. By the end of 1988 it was on sale in a nationwide mail-order catalog, complete with $1,000 worth of software for $995.

So, should I buy a computer? The conclusion has to be that you can get more for your money, or pay much less for the same thing, if you can wait a year or two to buy the equipment you want. Again, the simple rule to follow is: Don't buy any technology until you absolutely need it.

HOW MUCH OF MY INCOME SHOULD I SPEND ON NEW TECHNOLOGY?

In our experience, one to five percent of your gross income is the most you should spend on the acquisition of new technology in any given year. If your purchase doesn't live up to your expectations about saving time and money, you will have spent an amount small enough not to cause havoc in your business. More than five percent begins to be difficult to live with, especially if the equipment doesn't turn out to be as beneficial as you expected. A one to five percent level means that, with a gross annual income of $50,000, you could afford to spend from $500 to $2,500 per year on the acquisition of new equipment. If you have either heavy accounts payable or business loans that you are servicing, you should stay at or below the one percent level.

RESOURCES

Software

Recommended Accounting Packages (as of 1988)
Double Entry for the IBM or Compatible, Solomon III. TLB, Inc., Great Valley Corporate Center, 267 Great Valley Parkway, Malvern, PA 19355; 215-644-3344.
Double Entry for the Apple Macintosh, Great Plains for the Macintosh. Great Plains Software, 1701 S.W. 38th Street, Fargo, ND 58103; 701-281-0550.
Single Entry for Either IBM, IBM Compatible or Apple Macintosh, Quicken. Intuit, 540 University Avenue, Palo Alto, CA 94301; 415-322-0590.

Office Equipment

The Execufold desktop letter folder is available from ADI Machines for Business, 20505 East Valley Blvd., Suite 112, Walnut, CA 91789, 714-594-0097. It can fold up to three sheets of 8-1/2-by-11-inch paper at a time.

8

Marketing

In any business, marketing your goods or services is absolutely crucial to success. Although many businesses have a part-time or even a full-time person who is responsible for getting the word out, in a one-person business there is only you. And because you are busily wearing the many hats under which you keep the business going, you may be tempted to delegate the marketing domain to a professional. Or worse, to place a few ads in the local paper and cross your fingers.

To many people marketing is synonymous with advertising, where supposedly you pay the fee and customers flock to your business. And the business that can't afford the fee is out of luck. The fact is that *advertising is the least successful means of getting the word out about your business.* It is so far down on the list of successful marketing strategies as to be borderline. So save your advertising money and rely on the best marketing strategy there is—personal recommendation.

Unlike in advertising, there is no hyperbole involved in stimulating personal recommendations. People recommend to others only what they have come to know and trust; they are well aware that their own reputation is implicated in any recommendation they make.

Although it is a big responsibility to make sure your business is the kind that customers will want to tell their friends about, it also feels good. In fact, positive word-of-mouth commentary is one of those mythical win-win situations. You win because you attract new customers. The new customers win because they are delighted with your excellent service or the high quality of your product. The person who cared enough to share the news about your business wins both your appreciation and that of their friend. And all this good feeling is absolutely free!

If you offer a quality product or service, it is relatively easy to design and carry out a dynamic marketing plan. Doing so can be one of the most rewarding and fun parts of your business.

To help you develop your own marketing plan, we have divided the process into three categories: (1) Decide who you are—create a clear description of what your business offers. (2) Decide who you want as clients—that is, decide who your market will be. (3) Devise a plan to attract that market.

YOUR BUSINESS IDENTITY
IN THIRTY-FIVE WORDS OR LESS

The first step in marketing is to be able to describe your business clearly. You should try to do this in thirty-five words or less. If you can say, "I advise small businesses with from one to ten employees, on management issues such as personnel, marketing strategies, time management, support services, and financial projections," then your friends and admirers can more readily, and with total confidence, refer prospects to you. For you, too, it's ideal to have this concise, well-thought-out description ready to tote out at parties or other social occasions, or in more formal networking situations.

When we suggest to clients that others might not really understand what they do, they usually give us a look of disbelief accompanied by the statement that "everyone knows what a photographer, consultant, or desktop publisher does." Occasionally a client has already worked out an excellent description, including their special market niche, and is ready to use this description to promote word-of-mouth recommendations. But this individual is rare. Most clients cannot come up with a description, and they scoff when we ask them to carry out the following homework assignment: ask ten people, including friends and family members, to describe exactly what service or product they think your business offers. The purpose of this assignment is to find out if those most likely to give referrals have more than a generic idea about the business. Is our client just "some sort of photographer" to them, or can they say with assurance, "Pat specializes in candid wedding photos and does a top-notch job of photographing children. You won't have to drag your kids to a studio—he'll come to your home."

Most clients return enlightened from this experience. Usually their friends, and sometimes even their spouses, have only a vague idea of what they do. Friends who wanted to recommend them, for instance, but who knew only that they were a business consultant, were put in the position of lamely telling others something like, "I know a really nice business consultant, but I don't know what she specializes in. Here's her name and number—you can call her and check." This is obviously not an inviting referral.

Before we interviewed Alexandra Hart for this book, we knew only that she was a desktop publisher. What exactly did that mean? Was our fantasy of desktop publishing applicable to her particular business? What did she actually offer? Who were her clients? We discovered that Alexandra designs business cards, logos, stationery, posters, and books. For no extra charge she will travel to clients' offices, thereby providing a much appreciated extra service. We can now give her name with confidence when someone asks for help in creating an image for a business or in designing a poster for a jazz festival.

INFORMATION AND PROFESSIONAL BUSINESSES

Once you can clearly state exactly what your business does, the next step is to think about how you can give specific information on aspects of your work that most people won't be familiar with. It helps if you think of yourself as a facilitator. For example, if you are an experienced realtor, you know that most clients haven't the faintest idea of the services you perform for them. Your thirty-five word description may explain that you are a "realtor specializing in bare-land sales and are very knowledgeable about the history of each parcel as well as surrounding acreage," but it doesn't answer the question, "What's a realtor going to do for me?" Your clients may harbor the notion that you sit at your desk most of the time, reading a good novel while waiting for escrow (whatever that is) to close so that you can hop a cruise ship to the Far East with all your profit. If you take the time to create a sheet outlining the procedures involved in the sale of land, and another on what is involved in a home purchase or sale, you will have an informed and appreciative client—a client who is much happier to pay your fee. More important, this understanding of what you do can foster trust. And from trust come referrals.

Paul Terry bases the marketing of his small business advisory service on the service and information he provides to everyone. When Paul gets an inquiry, he tries to "spend as much time on the phone with the new person as seems to be necessary. Within a minute or so I can pretty much tell if the contact is worth exploring or if the person is just grasping for information. If the person is just in the information-gathering stage, I will act as a resource rather than trying to sell myself. I have written four or five articles over the last few years on how to do simple marketing research and set up a business plan. I send these out as a matter of course if they can help someone."

People want to be informed, active participants in what they pay for. They are no longer willing to hand over their health, legal, real estate, banking, or accounting problems to an expert who will take care of everything. More and more clients seek out businesses that understand their need to be informed partners working with a service provider, one who explains everything and offers alternatives. These consumer demands are difficult for many professionals to deal with, but in a one-person business there is enough flexibility to convert rapidly from the old-fashioned paternalistic-maternalistic mode, to the new practice of being open with information.

INFORMATION AND RETAIL BUSINESSES

Informing and educating customers is not the exclusive province of the professional. More and more retail businesses are also demystifying their operations, and by doing so are attracting loyal customers. Examples of this trend are photo processing stores where the curious can observe film being developed, sushi bars where every detail of the meal preparation is performed just a few feet from the diner, and upholstery stores that combine show- and workroom in order to encourage interested customers to learn a bit about the process of re-covering a couch or chair.

Keith Yates Audio, located in midtown Sacramento, California, is a "kick off your shoes, make yourself comfortable, and enjoy the best sound systems available" business. Yates bases his top-of-the-line audio sales business on multiple sales over the long run, rather than on the traditional one-time, cheaper sales. He maintains a very low overhead, which enables him to carry the products he believes in. He doesn't discount and he doesn't advertise. Willing to spend hours with clients, he feels that the more people can know and appreciate music through education, the more he will have loyal customers.

Rainbow General Store, a twelve-year-old collective located in the Mission District of San Francisco, is an excellent model of how a retail store can build trust though providing information. To help expand customer awareness, the store posts signs in the produce section explaining the origin of all fruits and vegetables. If the produce is organic, they say so; if they are unsure of the origin, they pass on that information also. Customers to whom the purchase of "certified organic" produce is important can shop at Rainbow secure in the knowledge that what they are buying is not only free of pesticides, but also full of vital nutrients because it is grown on healthy soil. In the housewares section, signs explain both the ingredients and the health implications of a variety of cleansing agents. It feels good to be able to refer friends who value organic produce and nontoxic cleansers to Rainbow General Store.

CUSTOMER SELECTION

When you are new in business, any customer seems like a small miracle, and the notion that you could actually select customers seems like a fairy tale. After you have been in operation for a while, it becomes apparent that you actually are

Market Surveys

If you want to test a new business idea to find out how well it will sell, try doing a market survey. Your goal is to learn how many potential clients for your product or service inhabit the market you would like to focus on, and what the likelihood of their buying from you might be.

A market is the industry segment or geographical trading area in which you want to do business. If you want to open a bookstore in a big city, you might define your market as one of the city's neighborhoods. If you want to sell used books, your market would be consumers who prefer to buy used books.

Your market survey would also include information from industry publications and sources about the industry you would like to enter. It would help you learn the answers to such questions as: How many consumers does it take to support a used book store? How many people live in the neighborhood where I would like to locate? How many titles do I need to carry and how many square feet of shelf space are needed to put them on?

The steps in making your market survey include: (1) determining the boundaries of your market or trading area, (2) studying the population of this area to determine its potential buying characteristics, (3) finding out the purchasing power of the area, (4) getting some numbers on what businesses like yours are currently making from selling the product or service you want to offer, (5) making an educated estimate of the portion of those sales that you can reasonably expect to get.

You will have to turn to local sources and to the government to find much of this information. Maps of your trading area are available on a county and state basis from many chambers of commerce, city development commissions, or newspaper offices. Many local governments will have census tracts for your area as well. Publications like *Sales Management* magazine can also be helpful. Trade associations, business libraries, departments at universities, and market research firms are other sources of information.

---

attracting a certain kind of person. In fact, whether you are conscious of it or not, you are actually selecting more than eighty percent of your customers.

As computer and training consultant Bill Dale puts it, "When I started I was glad of any work, but rapidly, within the first year or two, I weeded out my client base. I have been working for myself for almost ten years now, and within limits choose the clients I want to work with. For instance, I do not work for anyone that I don't like or whose company I regard as not worth supporting."

A business selects its customers in a number of ways:

You select customers by the price you charge.

A consultant who charges $1,000 a day will attract large corporations that operate in terms of day rates and long-term projects. A consultant who charges $50 per hour will attract small businesses that require his or her services for an hour or two at a time over a period of several months.

You select customers by your pricing schedules.

A plumber with a $200 minimum will work primarily with construction contractors. An auto mechanic who offers a discount for large jobs will largely attract auto rental businesses rather than off-the-street clients.

You select customers by the type of service you offer.

A fine printer will appeal to the poetry and specialty book trade rather than to mass market publishers.

You select customers by rejection.

A female criminal lawyer might have a policy of refusing to defend accused rapists. A dentist might refer alcoholic and obese clients to a specialist because he feels unqualified to treat people with special gum and heart problems.

You select customers by your attention and concern.

Customers know when you like them and appreciate the special care you demonstrate by paying extra attention to their needs and idiosyncrasies.

The primary objective in the conscious selection of your customers is to provide your business with a variety of income sources. As discussed in chapter 3, Financial Strategies, having diverse sources of income is necessary to the financial health of your business because it assures you steady income. It also encourages you to upgrade your skills and to be prepared to respond to the changing nature of your business.

HOW TO ATTRACT THE CUSTOMERS YOU WANT

Before we tell you what works in getting the word out about your business, let's briefly discuss why advertising is ineffective.

The Myth of Advertising

Advertising is offensive, expensive, and in America more intrusive than in any other industrialized nation. Advertising has made consumers cynical because it amounts to paid-for propaganda that is neither trustworthy nor memorable. According to market research studies, only nine percent of television viewers can name the brand or even the product category they saw advertised one moment before. In other words, only nine percent of the viewers can remember if they saw an ad for a bra or a floor mop.

Occasionally ads do generate name recognition, which may or may not affect sales. The Edsel, for instance, was the most advertised product of its time. Everyone remembers the Edsel, of course, but no one bought the car.

For professionals, advertising has traditionally been considered sleazy. Until recently, in fact, a lawyer who advertised his or her services as being superior or

---

Testament to the Futility of Advertising

In the May 23, 1988 edition of *Newsweek*, Charles Leerhsen found himself unhappily assigned to report on the best 250 TV commercials of the last ten years. Leerhsen noticed that claims about superior products had all but vanished, being replaced instead by commercials for soft drinks, aspirin, cars, floor wax, and cosmetics that were basically interchangeable and that pictured people "excited merely about living."

Curious, Leerhsen interviewed Dave Vadehra, president of Video Storyboard Tests, a business that measures the effectiveness of television ads. According to Vadehra, "We've reached the point where no one, including the manufacturers, thinks there is a bit of difference between advertised products. And so no one says anything because no one can think of a claim that anyone will believe."

---

less expensive could be disbarred. This taboo is based on common sense, for who, after all, would choose a pediatrician, let alone a brain surgeon, based on the claims of an ad. Most people find the businesses that provide the important services in their life through personal referrals. Professionals are quite aware of this and have traditionally relied exclusively on word of mouth to attract new clients.

Listings—The First Place People Will Look for Your Business

It's important to distinguish between advertisements, which are constant bombardments over which you have little control, and listings of goods and services that customers seek. It is extremely important for the one-person business to be listed in all directories, or trade publications, and any place else where potential customers might expect to locate your services or products. Listings are a one-person business's most effective marketing tool for attracting customers. Unlike advertisements, which interrupt and irritate, listings are well-placed gems waiting to be discovered by potential customers. Listings are placed where customers expect to find out about your business—the Yellow Pages, the Silver Pages for older citizens, the Ethnic Yellow Pages, college bulletin boards, commercial directories, and even the bulletin board at your local laundromat or grocery store.

Photographer Norman Prince is listed in both *Literary Marketplace* and *Audio-Video Marketplace*, as well as all the standard reference books in his field. Norman has given careful thought to the probable places someone would search for the services he offers, and these listings have paid off for him.

"For years I resisted the careerism-in-arts attitude where both teachers and students are focused toward making a career of being an artist," explains fine artist Bill Morehouse. "As a student of art, and as a young teacher, art had nothing to do with the vagaries of profit and gain. In recent years, however, I have more aggressively pursued the connections that would lead to sales of my work. I am listed both in the white and yellow pages of the phone book, under 'African and

---

Caution: Are You Ready for More Clients?

Before you attempt to create your marketing plan based on personal recommendations, take a critical look at your business. Is it operating well enough to accommodate new customers? If you do attract a lot of new customers, will you still be able to satisfy your steady clientele? Many a business has been sunk by an influx of customers when it wasn't prepared to respond.

Bill Dale, computer and training consultant, bases his marketing on personal references and has this good advice to offer: "Do a small job very well first. Then go for the next one. Beware of trying to tie up a big deal before you know the business, before the client knows you, and before you know what is involved. You will end up regretting it!"

Contemporary Art.' Also I'm in an international art listing of artists and critics for all countries and cities. I am in the *New York Art Review.* I also belong to an alumni club."

MARKETING PLANS BASED ON PERSONAL RECOMMENDATION

Most of you patronize businesses that are well run and that consistently offer quality goods and excellent service. For the most part, you have learned about these businesses from the personal recommendations of your friends and family. It makes sense, then, to base your own one-person business marketing efforts on this same premise. When you focus on your customers and gain their trust, they will not only recommend you, they will remain loyal to you. And this repeat business is what one-person businesses thrive on.

The two things that promote personal recommendations better than anything else are high-quality goods and superior service. Custom satchel designer Teri Joe Wheeler puts it this way: "Since I do custom work, clients appreciate small touches that make my product unique. This tells my customers that they are special. It takes more time but it's worth it in the long run. People want some magic, something personal. They want to know their possessions have quality because it's part of their statement about who they are. And because I provide that kind of quality customers recommend me to others."

Paul Terry, small business advisor, puts it another way: "I am a success or failure based on the quality of the work I do. Perhaps ninety percent of my work, if not more, is direct referral from other clients. Every client I work with has to have a successful involvement with me, or sooner or later I'll be cutting my own throat."

Gift retailer Nadine Travinsky conducts her business according to the rule "The customer is number one." "I give all my attention to the customer," she says. "While explaining the taffy-making process, I let them know that my taffy has no preservatives or candy wax, and then I give them a sample. I love having people sample my taffy and other goodies. I give newlyweds special samples, and I think word has spread because I get newlyweds in here all the time. If someone buys something and they are unhappy, I ask them why. If the item is defective I send it back to the manufacturer. If there's any other reason, I refund their money and absorb the loss."

Catherine Campbell, a family-practice lawyer, also provides extra service to her clients. "I keep a three-by-five card on every client I have. When I close their case, I make a note to send them information relating to child support, spousal support, custody, or visitation issues. If a really good article appears in a legal journal or some popular publication, I package it up and send it to every person who has an active card. When I close their file, I send them a letter that says, 'Thank you for hiring me; I hope you are satisfied. I will be sending you articles or information as it becomes available on the following subjects: . . .'"

Dr. Tom Ferguson operates on the same principle. "In general, I promote my services and products by being visible and by doing good work. I don't advertise. In the books that I write, there is a section in the back that tells people where they can write in for catalogs or related publications. This is a good marketing tool. Also, when I give seminars I take a more active role than most speakers do by getting involved, when possible, with the basic structure of the conference. I am very willing to plan the whole one- or two-day workshop, so that what I'm offering can take place in a setting that will be more meaningful to the participants. Whenever I'm doing a weekend seminar I like to offer a session where people are encouraged to break up into special-interest groups of their own choosing, without any leaders. I feel that for a lot of health professionals, the best thing that happens at these events is meeting their peers. It's important for people to link up. Equally important is to have representatives of local self-help and self-care agencies come and explain what they're about. Then it's not just someone from the outside coming in dispensing knowledge and just disappearing."

Checklist for Maintaining a Trustworthy Business

As we said above, personal recommendation is based on having the kind of business that others can trust. The following checklist excerpted from *Marketing Without Advertising* (Berkeley: Nolo Press, 1986) covers the points that any small business owner should pay special attention to.

1. My product or service is the best it can be.
2. I'm prepared to handle an increase in the number of customers generated by my marketing plan smoothly and efficiently.
3. The physical appearance of my business and of all my products, packaging, and other materials encourages customers to trust my management skills.
4. My pricing is clear, complete, and fair.

5. The people around me, including employees, suppliers, friends, and even those who dislike me, are treated as honestly and professionally as possible: If they don't agree with my business practices, they have clear and easy access to communicate with me.
6. I'm open about my finances and other aspects of my business.
7. I can clearly describe my business and so can most of my customers and suppliers.
8. My customers know as much as they want about my product or service, including what is superior and unique about the way I conduct my business.
9. Current and future customers can locate my business with ease.
10. Customers who have problems with me or my business are aware of my recourse procedure and feel they will end up satisfied.
11. I have a complete and current list of customers and my business community, and a file of activities that will be of interest to them.
12. I schedule and carry out marketing activities on a regular basis.

Now that you have developed a clear and precise way of describing what you do, have decided what kinds of customers you wish to work with, and are confident that your business is in good order, it's finally time to make a plan!

Mailing Lists—Your Primary Marketing Tool

Your list of prospects, clients, and suppliers is the most important marketing record you have. It is the basis for all your marketing events. The methods that follow are suitable for managing small lists of from a few to several hundred names. Whatever method you choose, make it easy to use, and keep it up to date.

Master-Sheet Method Bill Morehouse, fine artist, has assembled an impressive mailing list that includes people who have either purchased work or expressed interest, supportive friends involved in the art world, names of potential collectors given him by commercial galleries, and people who attend his showings. Because he wanted to handle his own promotions efficiently, in addition to what a gallery would do, Bill decided to enter his mailing list onto a master sheet, which he can photocopy onto labels.

His system works like this: Buy a box of 3-up Avery Labels, the kind that has three columns of eleven labels on an 8-1/2-by-11 backing sheet. Along with these labels comes a piece of paper with a grid laid out in exactly the same pattern as the labels. Place this sheet behind a blank piece of paper and then type all your names onto the outlined spaces. These are now your mailing list masters. When someone moves, merely cover the old address with a blank label and type over it directly onto your master.

Kate Bishop uses the same system as Bill. "I have a primary mailing list file of approximately four hundred names that I update with each new client. I keep this file very current. I also receive five hundred to a thousand labels from the Bridal Fair, a trade show where I rent a booth every year. I send these prospects and the people on my primary mailing list an invitation to my once-a-year sample sale. If the prospects from the Bridal Fair become clients, I add them to my primary list. If not, they receive no future mailings. This year I was super-busy and for the first time used a mailing service. I didn't receive a single response. This has never happened before, and I can't help but wonder if they actually sent the invitations. If I ever use a service again, I will include my own name as a control.

"Several years ago I needed to drum up some business, so I went through my list and wrote notes to clients I had not seen in a while, letting them know about some designs that might interest them. It worked. I learned from that experience that by writing a personal note reminding people about my business, I could be sure of getting responses."

Although you can handle up to a thousand names manually, once your list exceeds five hundred it's time to explore the cost to hire someone who would at least print your labels. When your list passes one thousand names, it's time for the services of a reliable mailing-list management business. This kind of service can create labels, stuff and label the envelopes, and take them to the post office much faster and with fewer errors than you can. It's just plain cost-effective.

Piggyback Method While the master-sheet method is a good way to handle mailing labels, if you need to keep track of details about each customer or supplier, add the piggyback method. Here's how it works: Purchase four-by-six-inch cards in yellow, red, and blue (or purple, pink, and green) along with a special kind of address label called "piggyback." Arbitrarily assign suppliers the yellow cards, prospects the red, and clients the blue. Using the piggyback labels, type the name, company, address, and phone number of each prospect. Affix these labels to the prospect (red) cards. For supplier (yellow) and client (blue) cards, omit the piggyback label but write the same information directly on the front of the cards. The reverse sides of the supplier and client cards can be used to record calls, visits, names of the people who referred them, dates of sales, etc. When a prospect (red) becomes a client (blue), give a cheer, peel off the piggyback label, and stick it onto a blue card. Any pertinent information contained on the red card can easily be saved by stapling the two cards together.

Effective Use of Your Mailing List Now that you have this up-to-date and easy-to-use mailing list system what do you do with it? Start using it. Get into the habit of mailing something of interest to everyone on your list at least four times a year. Perhaps your business can best communicate to customers through a newsletter. Or maybe you can send out a sample of your work, as photographer Norman Prince does.

You can also use your list to phone your customers to check how they are doing with the product you sold them or with the results of your last consulting project for them. Ask them if you can be of any further service. And be sure to ask if they can give you the names of one or two other people who might be interested in using your services or buying your products.

Let clients know, too, when anything new or exciting happens in your business that might be of interest to them. For example, if you are a massage professional who has just learned a new technique for alleviating the inflammation of tennis elbow, you would naturally call your carpenter, firewood dealer, and tennis player clients to share your excitement. This is the most direct and spontaneous approach to marketing and one that we encourage.

Marketing with your mailing list also includes informing clients about classes or product demonstrations you are giving, sending out promotional materials, and following up to make sure customers are satisfied. The following ideas are meant to inspire you to dream up appropriate, fun marketing events.

Samples and Demonstrations

Although it may seem farfetched that a one-person business could offer samples like big companies do, the basic idea is an excellent one. Kate Bishop, for instance, might want to send a recently dyed swatch of silk she is particularly proud of to her favorite customers. A caterer might call up some regular customers and offer to bring by her latest creation along with a price list. A printer might send out a sample of paper that he recently purchased in bulk and can offer at a good price.

Information is a different sort of sample you can share with people on your mailing list, something business consultant Paul Terry consistently pays attention to. Once a month or so, Paul reviews his most current inquiries, including referrals interested in his services and potential students interested in workshops. In addition, he reviews the folders of clients he has worked for in the last three months but hasn't recently communicated with. He calls these recent clients to see how they are getting along and to inquire whether they need any additional consultation. Often, even though Paul's clients did have further use of his services, they were too caught up in their day-to-day business to give him a call. Even if they didn't require any additional service, they all expressed appreciation for his taking the time to phone them.

Paul also maintains a computerized mailing list of about a hundred or so clients, two hundred students, and two hundred prospects to whom he occasionally sends out either a mailing to inform them of an upcoming workshop, or an interesting article about work he is involved in or considers relevant to the small business owner. He does this both to keep his list informed and to remind them that he is still interested in their business.

Celebrations

When Salli was the director of Farallones, an agricultural research institute engaged in alternative energy and organic gardening, her group was the host of a celebration-of-food event called *Taste of Spring*. This gala affair was sponsored by Wine Country Cuisine, a Sonoma County, California, food distributor, and by the San Francisco Culinary Academy. All of the organic growers and distributors in the greater Bay Area were invited, along with local gourmet chefs who either already used, or were interested in using, organic produce. Students from the San Francisco Culinary Academy prepared gourmet delights from locally grown fresh produce. What better way to show that carefully prepared fresh organic food has no equal?

Another kind of marketing event can be planned around a significant change in your business. When you move, change direction, purchase some significant office equipment, or meet an important goal, it is beneficial and fun to celebrate the changes. A celebration will remind people about your business and its part in their community. Whenever possible, celebrate at your place of business. If this is not possible, hold the event in a location that is strongly associated with your business. If you are a banking consultant, use a bank boardroom; if you sell art, use a gallery; and so forth. Keeping your community informed makes it easier for customers to continue referring other people to you. They will retain confidence in their referrals when they can participate in the growth of your business.

Equally effective is an event not directly related to your field or business at all, but which involves those who are in your field or customers of your business. Claude is an amateur photographer. He held an event in which he invited a half-dozen clients and suppliers who were also amateur photographers to exhibit their works together. Nearly 150 friends, peers, and clients attended the opening. It was a lot of fun, and everyone was surprised at the professional level of the work exhibited, even though it was an amateur show. Undoubtedly, the next time any of these people think about hiring a consultant, Claude will be likely to pop into their minds.

Promotional Material

Norman Prince has an agreement with the manufacturer of a high-quality color printing press to lithographically reproduce some of his photographs during trade show demonstrations. In exchange, Norman gets several thousand copies of these same photographs made into greeting cards or postcards. Several times a year, if you are on Norman's mailing list, you can look forward to receiving a small selection of these beautiful cards. Norman includes the following cover letter:

Dear (name):

Enclosed please find some cards with a photograph of mine from (wherever the photo was taken). This photograph was taken using (type of film, lens, filter and/or technique) for (client).

I hope that you enjoy these cards.

Sincerely,

Norman Prince

This is a wonderful marketing technique. The important point is that on the back of every one of these cards is an imprint reading "Norman Prince, Photographer, San Francisco, California." When you come across this card, months after receiving it, or if one of your friends or clients sees it and wants to know who did the work, the name is clearly there. But this wouldn't be an effective label unless Norman also made sure he was listed in the San Francisco phone directory, which he does.

Anyone who sells products to retail outlets has probably encountered the typical retailer's resistance to letting you label your product with your address and phone number. Naturally you want to make sure that the customer can continue to buy your product should the retailer drop it or go out of business. Most retailers won't object to a simple name, city, and state label such as dress designer Kate Bishop uses. Kate told us, "I went to a fancy business consultant who charged me $300 and gave me no other useful information except that, since my dress labels said 'San Francisco, California,' I should be listed in the directories of San Francisco, Marin County, and as many other adjacent counties as I could afford. Otherwise the label would be useless. It was very good information, well worth $300."

Judgment Cards

"Judgment cards" are a special vehicle first introduced to us by career counselor Shali Parsons. A friend of his who was looking for bookkeeping work had asked him for help. Shali recommended that she write down a clear description of exactly the work she was looking for. Next he suggested that she type this description onto four-by-six-inch note cards and pass them out to people in a position to refer work to her. The note cards made it easy for friends and associates to remember her when someone asked if they knew of a bookkeeper. The clear description on the card provided potential clients with a level of judgment regarding her skills that would otherwise have been impossible to obtain without calling her first.

Helen Hendricks, a therapist, uses a similar judgment card that includes the statement "You're Not Crazy." in bold print at the top. There follows a list of the symptoms of psychological stress and the conclusion that just because you are feeling some of these symptoms doesn't mean you've necessarily gone over the edge (*see Figure* 8.1).

Many small businesses we're acquainted with have used judgment cards to good effect. The basic rules for creating a good judgment card are simple:

- It should have a list of at least five things that would help a client judge your knowledge of your field.
- These five things should be easily applied to you.
- The product or service that you offer should be absolutely clear.
- The information should be presented in an interesting enough way that people will want to save it.

The note card format together with the interesting information encourages people to pin a judgment card on the bulletin board or near the phone, or to keep it in a wallet or purse for future reference. The small cards are also easy to pass from person to person. They can be like a mini-brochure but are much quicker to read (*see Figure* 8.2).

Marketing Calendars of Events

Now that you are looking at your business with marketing events in mind, it is time to purchase a big wall calendar and to start scheduling these events. When you are busy, it is tempting to neglect marketing. Inevitably, then, business will slack off, and you will wish you had events lined up. Plan events throughout the year, leaving enough time in between to make them fun rather than a chore.

Once you have decided on dates, prepare a worksheet for each event detailing every important step and deadline—when the invitations must be at the printers, when the press releases should go out, when the flowers must be picked up, etc. Note all of these deadlines on your oversized wall calendar and get ready for your new customers!

PUBLICITY

Sooner or later the idea of attracting some favorable publicity for your business will begin to seem like a good idea. In a few rare cases you might be asked to appear on national TV or radio, and you would have to decide whether you could handle the resulting anxiety and attention. Although this once-in-a-lifetime publicity shot might be something to tell your grandchildren about, unless you are a writer or entertainer it wouldn't do much to promote your business. Much more important to your business is publicity sought within your own community as part of a well-thought-out marketing campaign.

Publicity seems the mysterious province of a lucky few, something out of reach for a car mechanic, hairdresser, accountant, or doll restorer. Besides, you

Ten Remedies for
WRITER'S BLOCK

1. Call a friend and explain where you're stuck.
2. Go for a walk.
3. Draw a "concept map," putting each idea, sub-idea, and pre-idea in a bubble and connecting the bubbles with arrows.
4. Give up temporarily.
5. Listen to music.
6. Write about how frustrated and stuck you are, ~~ing plenty of obscenities.~~
   ~~osite of what you're trying to say.~~
   ~~ce—write your idea~~
   ~~nal Enquirer~~

YOU'RE NOT CRAZY.

Does this sound familiar?

☐ *You want to exert more control over your life.*

☐ *You have concerns about your social/sexual life.*

☐ *You have recently started or ended a relationship.*

☐ *You have a new baby and feel overwhelmed.*

☐ *You've been promoted to a new job, or . . .*

☐ *You or your mate have lost a job.*

☐ *You've recently lost a parent or friend.*

☐ *You or your family have had repeated illnesses.*

☐ *You want to learn about your stress and ways of utilizing it more effectively.*

M.F.C.C. M2457

You're not crazy if one of these life changes is getting you down.

Helen Jensen Hendricks R.N. (Ph.D. candidate) is a licensed Marriage, Family, Child Counselor who consults with business, industry and education. Call her. You can maximize your potential and manage life stress.

San Francisco

Insurance accepted.

Figs. 8.1 and 8.2   Judgment Cards

have also heard of people who have gotten hurt by bad publicity—"bad" meaning that you are quoted inaccurately, your business is presented in a misleading way, or worse. Yet, people in the media are like people everywhere. Most are kind and want to do a good job of presenting your story to their public. After all, you are their bread and butter; too many inaccurate stories, and the reporter or newscaster will be looking for another job.

The media are hungry for interesting stories. All you must do is gain their attention. Once you have it, respect those who want to spread the good news about your business: Be truthful, don't blow your own horn too much, and don't overuse them for your personal gain.

Quotes from an "Expert in the Field"

Becoming known as an expert in your field is a big plus in attracting favorable publicity. If you can, write a column for your local newspaper or have a weekly radio spot where people call in with questions relevant to your business. People will begin to look to you for information. Ever notice how some people's names seem to show up repeatedly in your hometown newspaper? That's because the media is on an eternal deadline, and they will naturally call you, the "expert," because they don't have to worry about the validity of your contribution. Writing an interesting response to the letters-to-the-editor section of your newspaper or trade journal is another way to become known as an expert in your field. Remember to identify your business and location.

If you get on a television or radio show or find yourself being asked penetrating questions by a local reporter, remain calm. Most one-person businesses love talking about their work. So just concentrate on what you love and not yourself or what you look like on the TV monitor. Usually, you can relax in the company of a professional media person, whose job it is to provide a good show or write an interesting article. Media professionals are dedicated to providing their audience with entertainment and information and they know their business. All you have to do is share yours.

Whether you are a foot doctor, a plant tender, a drum repair person, or a stained glass restorer, there are people interested in your business. These two facts: You are interesting to others, and the media has a lot of time and space to fill, should give you all the confidence you need to go for it!

Once you have made it through your first interview, don't sit around staring at your clipping, or wear out your tape of the show. To be effective, publicity must be carried out on a regular basis and is just one part of your marketing efforts. Make sure your business can handle the brief flurry of inquiries that is bound to result from, say, a feature story in the Sunday paper. Keep in mind that maintaining superior service, for old customers as well as new, must always be your first consideration. The best strategy is to maintain a regular, low-profile exposure punctuated with an occasional bit of hullabaloo.

Should You Hire a Publicist?

Publicists are like bookkeepers. There are a lot of fine ones around and you can benefit from their expertise. But a one-person business should use both sparingly. Just as it may be a good idea to hire a bookkeeper to help you set up a workable system, it may be beneficial to hire a publicist for a few hours to help you formulate some of your ideas and to provide you with contacts. But it's your business, and no one knows it better than you or can talk about it as enthusiastically. Besides, you probably don't have a lot of money to spare. Although a publicist is invaluable for some businesses, such as for an author planning a promotion tour, for the typical one-person business it's definitely not necessary to have one on retainer or hire anyone to run the whole show.

RESOURCES

Accounting Corporation of America, *Barometer of Small Business* (1929 First Avenue, San Diego, CA 92112).

Robert Morris Associates, *Annual Statement Studies* (Philadelphia National Bank Building, Philadelphia, PA 19107).

Michael Phillips and Salli Rasberry, *Marketing Without Advertising* (Berkeley, California: Nolo Press, 1986).

Laura Sachs, *Do-It-Yourself Marketing for the Professional Practice* (Englewood Cliffs, New Jersey: Prentice-Hall, Inc., 1986).

Small Business Administration, *Sales Forecasting for Small Business* (Publication 1.10/2:2, No. 48).

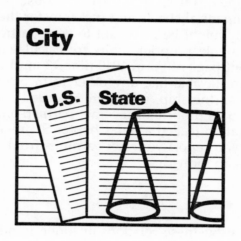

9

Legal Matters

All businesses are set up according to certain broad legal definitions—basically as sole proprietorships, partnerships, or corporations. A one-person business can be any of these, but by far the largest number are sole proprietorships. This chapter addresses each business form and some of its tax implications. Other legal details you need to be concerned about include your obligations toward anyone you hire, zoning ordinances that may affect where you can work, and permits and licenses required by some state and local authorities.

THE LEGAL FORM OF YOUR BUSINESS

In business you usually start off as a sole proprietor, regardless of whether you have employees or run your business with a spouse. You may, however, form a partnership or a corporation by using certain legal steps; you can operate several different businesses with one or more as sole proprietorships and the others as partnerships or corporations.

Sole Proprietorship

The definition of sole proprietor is primarily meaningful in a tax context. It means that you file a federal Schedule C (Form 1040), "Profit or (Loss) from Business or Profession," in addition to your Form 1040, "U.S. Individual Income Tax Return." The categories of the Schedule C are similar to those in the monthly records many small businesses use, and it is easy to use the same expense categories in your monthly financial sheets and just transfer the yearly totals to your tax forms (although many might be irrelevant to your particular business.)

Net earnings from a sole proprietorship are calculated on Schedule C and then reported on the front page of Form 1040 (line 13 on the 1987 version). These business net earnings are taxable like any other form of earnings. The same is true for earnings from a partnership, which are recorded on an adjacent line (line 17 on the 1987 version). Sole proprietor income, partnership income, and income from one kind of corporation (called a Sub-Chapter S) are all treated for tax purposes in the same way; you report your net earnings from them and pay regular income taxes on them as an individual.

Partnership

A partnership is any business relationship done jointly with other people, except as a corporation. From a tax point of view, a partnership is almost non-existent. The only thing required is the filing of a simple annual notice of the revenue distributed to the partners (called a K-1). To do a K-1 a tax ID number is needed, which can be obtained simply by filing a request for a federal tax ID number.

From a legal point of view, a partnership is a real entity, whether a written partnership agreement exists or not. Unfortunately, for many small businesses a written document does not exist. Partnerships should always be in writing. The key parts to note are (1) the purpose of the partnership, (2) the distribution of earnings and responsibilities, (3) dissolution procedures, and (4) a mediation clause. See Figure 9.1 for an example of a good mediation clause. Also, an excellent reference book on this subject is *The Partnership Book* (Berkeley, California: Nolo Press, 1987).

One form of partnership exists solely for investment purposes—the limited partnership. It is made up of one or more partners who run the business, called the general partners, and the people who contribute only money, called the limited partners. The designation "limited" means that these people are legally liable for any actions of the partnership only to the degree of business ownership that their contribution of money represents. They must also have nothing to do with running the business. If the business is forced to settle a lawsuit, they can lose the money they invested.

Fig. 9.1   Partnership Agreement

PARTNERSHIP AGREEMENT

==

This partnership agreement is entered into and effective as of
_____, 19 _____, by Michael P. Stein (Mike), and Claude F.
Whitmyer (Claude), "the partners".

The partners desire to form a general partnership under the laws of the state
of California for the purposes and on the terms and conditions stated in this
agreement.

---- BODY OF AGREEMENT WOULD BE HERE ---

XII. DISPUTE RESOLUTION

    A. Claude F. Whitmyer and Michael P. Stein, the partners, agree that
any dispute arising out of this agreement or the partnership
business shall be resolved by mediation. This includes the
partners, employees, clients and suppliers. The partners are aware
that mediation is a voluntary process, and pledge to cooperate
fully and fairly with the mediator in an attempt to reach a
mutually satisfactory compromise of any dispute.

    B. The mediators shall be chosen from the list of friends, associates
and advisors in ADDENDUM 4. Each partner will choose one mediator,
and the two mediators shall choose a third.

    C. If any party to a dispute feels it cannot be resolved by the
partners themselves, he/she shall notify both partners, in writing.

    D. Mediation shall commence within 30 days of this notice of request
for mediation.

    E. Any decision reached by the mediation shall be reduced to writing,
signed by all parties, and will be binding on them.

Fig. 9.1   Partnership Agreement (*continued*)

F. If the parties cannot reach a decision by mediation, the dispute

shall be arbitrated under the terms of this clause.

1. The arbitration shall be carried out by a single arbitrator,
    who shall be agreed upon by the parties to the dispute. If
    the parties cannot agree on the arbitrator, the arbitrator
    shall be selected by the three persons who acted as
    mediators to this dispute.

2. The cost of arbitration shall be borne by the parties, as
    the arbitrator shall direct, as part of the arbitration
    award.

3. The arbitration award shall be conclusive on the parties,
    and shall be set in such a way that a formal judgment can be
    entered thereon in the court having jurisdiction over the
    dispute if either party so desires.

---- MORE AGREEMENT WOULD FOLLOW ----

ADDENDUM 4: FRIENDS, ASSOCIATES AND MENTORS WHO HAVE AGREED TO ACT AS
             MEDIATORS.

CLAUDE: Greta Alexander, Clark Berry, Martin Hamilton, Tom Hargadon,
         Joan McIntosh, Finley Peavey

MIKE: Richard Silberman, Peter Horn, Tom Frankel, Diane Kaufman,
         Wayne Canterbury

Corporation

The corporation has the legal quality of a living being. It can be taxed, sued, forced into bankruptcy, and adopted by another being (in a merger). It differs in that it can't die of old age, and it can be sold.

If you are considering incorporation, keep the following points in mind. Because a corporation can be sued, the law generally protects the owners of the corporation, as individuals, from suit for the same actions. Even if you and the corporation are really one and the same, which is only possible in a few states such as California and Maryland, the corporation is sued for its actions and only its assets are vulnerable in a settlement. The exception is if the corporation is improperly formed in the first place or if you fail to hold regular board meetings, keep good minutes or otherwise run it improperly. As a one-person business owner, it is wise to remember that although forming a corporation may protect you from liability for the corporation's actions, you must still defend yourself against the suit, which can bankrupt you personally. A more useful perspective is to focus on the tax benefits of incorporation, which under the Tax Reform Act of 1986 begin to occur after you are generating about $300,000 or more in annual income.

Because it is taxed, you have to file separate tax returns for the corporation to the state and federal government. Corporate taxes are calculated on net earning before payments to the owner, and these earnings are then taxed again as personal income to the owner—in other words, you are taxed twice. The salary to an owner is taxed only as salary. The exception to this rule is a form of corporation called the Sub-Chapter S Corporation which is allowed to pass profits through to the stockholders, where they are taxed only once as stockholder income.

Tax laws for corporations change occasionally and unexpectedly. In addition to the concerns already mentioned, you should note two important items that influence some people in their decision to incorporate. As the tax laws change, either of these items may change in such a way as to harm or benefit your business.

1. Corporations have a minimum level of net earnings on which they pay taxes, and you may expect to earn below that level.
2. Certain expenses related to health insurance, life insurance, and pensions that are not deductible as business expenses to sole proprietorships or partnerships are deductible as business expenses to corporations.

Corporations can be bought and sold in whole and in part a little more readily than other forms of business. Corporate ownership is in the form of stock certificates, and these can be traded without affecting the business. The stock certificates may contain provisions requiring all other existing shareholders to bid on stock before it is sold to new people. The corporation can also promise to buy the stock back for a fixed price in the future, and retail markets can be created to sell corporate stock. (In the latter case, be careful because Securities and Exchange Commission laws govern all aspects of stock sales, even the "prospect" of a "stock offering" to another person. The lawyers who deal with this issue are expensive but should be consulted if you are considering selling stocks.)

Relative Merits

In the final analysis, for most one-person businesses the sole proprietorship represents the simplest form to choose and maintain. A partnership may be beneficial from time to time when collaboration for a longer period seems desirable. A corporation requires the most work to maintain, and its true benefits do not begin to show themselves until you are generating a larger amount of income than most small businesses anticipate.

LEGAL OBLIGATIONS WITH NONEMPLOYEES

For tax purposes, when you hire part-time workers you may have to treat them as employees, whether they really are or not. If so, you will have to withhold taxes for them and pay several forms of tax in addition to the wages you pay them. To avoid this, you should understand the way in which federal and state agencies view the different individuals you might hire to work with you. Then you can protect yourself by establishing clear relationships.

Independent Contractors

Here are some excerpts on independent contractor status from the *Federal Tax Coordinator*, a publication used by accountants to stay current on tax laws.

> In general, an individual who is subject to the control and direction of another only as to the result of his work, and not as to the means, is an independent contractor and not an employee. Physicians, lawyers, dentists, veterinarians, contractors, subcontractors, public stenographers, auctioneers, and others who follow an independent trade, business, or profession in which they offer their services to the public are usually independent contractors according to the Treasury regulations.
>
> A "free-lance worker" may or may not be subject to withholding. If the relationship between such a worker and the person paying for his services is such that the latter has the right to tell him what kind of work to do and how to do it, the worker will be considered an employee. But a person who works at home on a piecework basis is considered an independent contractor if he is subject to another's control only as to the result of the services and not as to the method of performing them. (He's nevertheless subject to FICA withholding.)

A general contractor wasn't the employer of the employees of its subcontractor even though it occasionally gave instructions directly to these employees and the subcontractor generally followed its advice as to hiring and firing. The subcontractor had full control of its employees and the fact that it chose to defer to the general contractor for business reasons didn't give the latter control.

Similarly, a subcontractor was an independent contractor and not a joint venturer with the general contractor where the latter only advanced funds which would be due at the completion of the job; shared in profits only because it advanced funds; didn't share losses or have any personal liability; and didn't have common management and control.

In determining whether an individual was an independent contractor, a district court considered the following factors:

1. Whether the person receiving the benefit of the service has the right to control the manner and method of performance;
2. Whether the person rendering the service has a substantial investment in his own tools or equipment;
3. Whether the person rendering the service undertook substantial costs to perform the services;
4. Whether the person performing the service had an opportunity for profit dependent on his managerial skill;
5. Whether the service rendered required special training and skill;
6. The duration of the relationship between the parties;
7. Whether the service performed is an integral part of the recipient's business, rather than ancilliary position;
8. Whether the person rendering the service had a risk of loss;
9. The relationship which the parties believed they created;
10. Whether or not the person who performed the services offered such services publicly and practiced an independent trade;
11. Whether the custom in the trade or industry was for the service to be performed on an independent contractor or employee basis;
12. Whether the person who received the benefit of the service held the right to discharge without cause the person who performed the service;
13. Whether the person who performed the services had the right to delegate his duty to others.

Conceivably, an individual may be both an employee and an independent contractor with respect to the same party. If, for example, an employee, in addition to his regular work, contracts with his employer to sell the company's product on his own time, he may be considered to be an independent contractor with respect to the work performed under that contract. At the same time, of course, the wages paid him for his regular work as an employee would be subject to withholding.

Many agent-drivers, full-time salesmen, and industrial homeworkers are treated as employees under Social Security, even though they are independent contractors under the control test. However, "control" remains the test for withholding purposes. Such an individual is still exempt from income tax withholding as an independent contractor if he is not subject to another's control.

Workers who are not employees can be roughly grouped into four categories: casual labor, rented labor, partner, or independent contractor.

Casual labor is any person whom you hire to do a short, one-time job, such as chopping wood, hauling an old sofa, or washing windows. You don't pay them very much, and you probably don't hire them more than once.

Rented labor is a person you get from a temporary agency such as Kelly Girl, Manpower, or Daisy; he or she is really an employee of the agency. You may hire temporary personnel for an hour or a month and you may have them come back repeatedly. But they are still not your employees.

Partner refers to a real partner in a legal sense.

True *independent contractors* include your lawyer, accountant, foot surgeon, and chimney sweep. They have their own businesses and their own tools, are their own boss, and almost always have clients other than you. The rules and regulations about who is and who is not an independent contractor are numerous. On the list of jobs or occupations that have been denied withholding exemption you will find many of the same jobs or occupations that have been granted the exemption. However, the general guidelines are pretty clear. For additional information, get Circular E, "Employers Tax Guide," from the IRS, or you can file Form SS-8 to obtain a ruling on a specific case. Your best insurance is to ascertain that all of the independent contractors working for you act like individual businesses. Ask them if they keep books and regularly file a Schedule C, on which what you pay them is included. Explain to them that you will be filing Form 1099 (explained below) to report your payments to them to the IRS.

The biggest problem of the independent contractor versus employee issue usually comes up after you have stopped working with someone and you find out that he or she has filed an unemployment claim. Suddenly you are faced with an audit about your practices regarding independent contractors. To avoid this, be sure to discuss the issue openly with any subcontractors about whom you have doubts. Explain that, as independent contractors, they will not be eligible for unemployment compensation. This kind of frank discussion should give you a feeling for whether they understand what being an independent contractor means, and whether you are going to have a problem later. Try to hire only people who seem to take being in business for themselves seriously enough to file all the correct tax forms, and who are unlikely to file for unemployment later.

The government keeps tabs on the amount of money paid to independent contractors by having you report it on Form 1099. Every January you are required by federal tax law to fill out 1099 forms and mail them to each independent contractor you hired in the previous year. You will need to include their tax ID number or Social Security number on the form. The only exceptions are if (1) your total payments to them were under $600 during the year, or (2) they are a corporation.

In preparation, it is a good idea to track the money you spend on any independent contractor as you go along, so that you don't have to burn the midnight oil in January to get the forms out. You might keep a separate file labeled 1099, and when a payable is going to someone for whom you will have to write a 1099 in January, you can drop a copy of the check or invoice into that file. You must also remember to forward a copy of all 1099s to the IRS; you use Form 1096 to do this.

ZONING RESTRICTIONS

If you run your business out of your home, you risk violating local residential zoning ordinances. Zoning is radically different in every single community and city in the U.S. In some exclusive suburbs with gates and guards, a graphic artist with a worktable in the house would be in violation of the code and subject to a $5,000 penalty. By contrast, in the back counties of some states you could sell purebred horses out of your living room with no problem—at least no zoning problem.

Because of this national variation it is important to get the facts. Don't assume they are logical. Zoning is based on history, political structures, and social perceptions, not logic or necessity.

To get good advice, you should talk to a local person with political and zoning experience, and give a few statistics about your operation. These include how many people a week come to your house and where they park; how often you have UPS package pickups and deliveries; and whether any visible equipment used in your business (such as a 300-foot antenna, or an 18-wheel truck) is located near you.

If what you do is not legal for the zone you live in, learn what the penalties are and then decide whether to ignore the law or not. Always assume that at some time you will be reported; you don't want to have to move at a time not of your choosing.

LICENSES, PERMITS, AND FEDERAL ID NUMBER

Many cities and counties require that you obtain a permit or license to operate. Check with your local government to find out whether your business is subject to this requirement. You may also need to get a license to do business from the state government. In addition, all businesses, even one-person businesses, are required to have a federal ID number. In many cases you may use your personal Social Security number for this purpose. To obtain a separate federal ID number (called an employer identification number, or EIN) file Form SS-4 with the IRS.

FICTITIOUS NAMES

If you wish to operate your business using a name other than your own, you may be required by your state or local government to file a DBA (doing business as) or statement of fictitious business name. This usually involves registering with the appropriate government agency and then publishing your intent to use the name in a local newspaper. Regulation may vary depending on where you live, so check with your state or local government.

REGISTRATION FOR SALES TAX

Most states, and some local governments, require you to apply for a permit to sell taxable products or services. This regulation can apply to wholesalers, retailers, or consultants. You may be required to make a security deposit against future payments for the taxes you are supposed to collect.

RESOURCES

Denis Clifford and Ralph Warner, *The Partnership Book* (Berkeley, California: Nolo Press, 1986).

Internal Revenue Service, *New Business Tax Kit.* Contains information about taxes and tax forms as well as a comprehensive guide to federal taxation of small businesses. Available in local IRS offices.

Time off

10

Emotional Support Systems

A one-person business can fail for a number of reasons, a few of them obvious, such as lack of competence in your chosen field, lack of persistence, and severe illness. The most common reason, though, and the least discussed, is emotional stress. Emotional health is not usually considered a factor in the success or failure of a business. It's as if life must be compartmentalized and a death in the family dealt with only at night or on weekends. No matter what happens, come Monday morning it's time for a stiff upper lip. Pretending that emotions have no effect on business is naive, and it definitely won't work in a one-person business.

A one-person business has to rely heavily on self-starting energy, which is usually in abundance unless things go wrong on an emotional level. If you are losing sleep worrying about something, there is no boss to pressure you into getting on with the day's business, and little motivation to get up and attend to what suddenly seems like an overwhelming amount of details.

Only part of your business has immediate and direct rewards, such as talking to an enthusiastic customer, giving a well-received speech, or mailing off your manuscript. Much of the work involves dealing with administrative details and requires pure self-starting energy—the kind that is drained by depression, grief, sorrow, or self-pity. Catastrophic events over which you have no control are bound to happen. Your spouse may leave, friends may die, illnesses may occur. A one-person business owner has to acknowledge this and arrange for some sort of support in advance. The bills have to be paid, the late supplier checked on, the telephone messages retrieved and answered. There is no one to take responsibility but you.

As property manager Diane Stuart explains, "You have to have a real drive that comes from inside and propels you to do things. Once you reach that level of enthusiasm about what you're doing, you'll put out whatever energy it takes to make it work. Without that self-starting energy it's very difficult."

Before the industrial revolution it might not have been necessary to make observations such as these. Many people used to belong to communities that included support structures. But the advent of large-scale manufacturing brought a decline in this kind of community structure. Now when we encounter people who have rebuilt support structures around themselves, we call them "extended families." It is as if we see the nuclear family—mother, father, and children—as the basic social unit. But in fact it has been this for only about the past 200 years.

Because the support of the naturally larger family and the clan or community has been lost to us, we must consciously recreate it. As business consultant Paul Terry puts it, "Juggling the balls of how you run your business, maintaining your relationships, getting some exercise, and preserving some kind of spiritual aware-ness can be hard. Sometimes you feel like your business is working, but you never get any exercise; or sometimes you are getting a lot of exercise but ignoring your business; or putting a lot of energy into your relationships but not finding the time for contemplation of your spiritual life. Being a one-person business, you sometimes have to create your own environment, rather than having an environment created for you."

Fortunately, there are many ways to create this supportive environment and maintain the necessary self-starting energy to run a one-person business. In this chapter we will discuss some of the typical dangers and concerns connected with running a one-person business and suggest ways of dealing with them.

STABILIZATION THROUGH ROUTINE

If you go to bed and get up at a different time each day, never eat regular food at a regular time, have no regular exercise, and in general lack any kind of dependable rhythm to your life, then you are bound to experience wide emotional swings.

On the other hand, if you decide on a certain routine and then simply do what needs to be done regardless of how you feel, you will soon find your emo-tions stabilizing. If this sounds too simplistic, you can easily check it out. Start by cooking yourself one meal, with forethought and awareness, at the same time each day. It doesn't take much observation to discover what psychologists have known for many years—emotions follow behavior.

After you have gotten into the routine of a regular meal, add a daily constitutional or walk. Fifteen minutes is enough. Keep watching what happens to your mood swings as your routine builds momentum. Most people report an amazing stabilizing effect.

Our clients have found many ways to ensure emotional stability in their lives. Nadine Travinsky, for example, uses the requirements of her home and gift shop to dictate her routine. "I get up every morning at the same time, make my husband breakfast, do the routine chores, and am at the shop by ten. I leave at five except on weekends when I stay until six. Except for making up my money bag for the next day, I relax in the evening. I start out with the same amount of cash every day, so when I make up my money bag for the next day, I know what my profit was for today. Sometimes I work on my books in the evening also."

Shirley, who runs a word processing business from her home, relies on a regular session in the garden each morning. Sandy, a successful potter, does meditation every morning, and every Saturday drops in for lunch at her nearby Zen Center. Five days a week, Michael runs at 6:00 A.M. Afterward he exercises, takes a warm shower followed by a cold one, and then goes to a coffeehouse to meet with friends before going to work. Charles, a computer consultant, gets up at the last minute, drinks several cups of strong coffee, and rushes to work. After dinner he always smokes an expensive cigar, and he spends his last waking hour reading up on his latest intellectual pursuit. (We include Charles to make it obvious that "healthy" and "spiritual" are not the only reasonable ways to build routine.)

The range of options is great: exercise, meditation, therapy, yoga, meeting with friends, as well as reading, eating and even smoking a cigar. The key is to give high priority to the need for routine. Different people require more routine than others. For some, doing something once a week is enough. For others, it must be every day.

Observing and modifying the effect that routine has on your daily life is an activity well worth engaging in. David Reynolds, in his book, *Constructive Living*, explains it like this:

> America is a land of freedom, we say. Yet all around us are restrictions on what we can do. Only designated persons can prescribe medicine, only certain drugs can be taken legally, streets should be crossed only when the traffic light is green, children under a certain age cannot work for wages, it is impolite to sneeze in someone's face, social greetings are required at parties, we are expected to speak on one level of formality to our bosses and another way to our friends. We are not entirely free in what we do, of course. And no one really wants to live an absolutely unfettered life. Children who are given too much leeway are miserable; they actually seek limits and direction from adults. Mentally disturbed people also seem more comfortable when a warm but firm hand limits the boundaries of their "crazy" behavior. Even artists are never truly free.

They voluntarily take on the limits of the medium they use, the style they employ, the model, the patron, time constraints, the question of cost, and so on.
We are able to operate within these limits, even to enjoy some of them, because our behavior is controllable in a way that our feelings are not. There is a very special satisfaction for the Artist of Living who works within life's limits to produce a fine self-portrait. The more control we develop over our actions, the more chance we have of producing a self we can be proud of.

People find many ways to promote emotional stability through regular daily routines. And when you're your own business, doing this takes on a special meaning.

WAYS TO OVERCOME ISOLATION

Every owner of a one-person business contends with isolation. It's always going to be there, and you must give it some thought to make sure you don't find yourself staring miserably at the walls one day, with nowhere to turn. Isolation can be partially overcome by occasional get-togethers with peers or by structuring time to get out of the office every day, so that you will see other people. But it's also important to take a hard look at your personality to see if you really can work alone. If you are super-gregarious, or spent many years in a friendly office situation, you might decide that a shared business space is for you.

A wide variety of shared business space exists, from business "incubators" on one end to full-service offices on the other. The different services fall into four major groupings:

- Business or office space with services and office equipment
- Space and services rented to a group of businesses that are related or that share clients in some way
- Services, shared clients, and some kind of an advisory service
- Services, shared clients, an advisory service, and start-up financing

All of these arrangements usually include secretary and receptionist services, copy machines, and reception and meeting areas. They sometimes include computers, laser printers, facsimile machines, bookkeepers, accountants, and business lawyers. The last two are sometimes called "incubators." An incubator is any arrangement that offers some combination of financing and advice. Financing usually takes the form of a subsidy built into the rent for the primary purpose of helping businesses get started. The subsidy may cease after a fixed period of time, or after the business gets going. Incubators are usually sponsored by local economic development agencies. Check with your area government to see if any exist near you.

Each of these basic forms has advantages and disadvantages. The big disadvantage is the limited number of locations where you can find this type of business service. Among the advantages, aside from solving the isolation problem, is the smaller amount of money you need to invest in office equipment and office support services because you are sharing. Also, you often get access to meeting rooms or other facilities you might not otherwise be able to afford.

Catherine Campbell, a family attorney, has her office in a shared space that includes some services. "My business is self-contained. I don't share my economic setup with any other attorneys, and I have no employees. I do share space with a group of other attorneys, and a receptionist and common secretarial pool. Within the office I have a 'one on one' relationship which is infinitely valuable for someone like me who has ethical and emotional problems in her work. It's just a very close, intimate friendship in the office that is available to me at any hour I need it. It is essential, the protein of everything there. It would be hard for me to live with the isolation I think I would experience if I didn't have that friendship within the office. In addition to that we have a professional relationship. We meet to discuss issues that come up in the office context. It would be difficult to deal with the internal politics of the office and the structural problems of the office and common needs and experiences that occur without that friendship."

If you only need occasional use of meeting space or support services, you can get them from companies that specialize in meeting-space rentals or office services. You can join a local professional or networking group for your business field. Teri Joe Wheeler, a designer of fine satchels, has located her home and studio on an isolated rural property a few hours drive from San Francisco. "I go for a run every morning, and on my run I check the phone machine, which is about a half mile from my studio. Then I spend some time enjoying the garden before going to work. Although I lack the access of people who live in an urban environment, I get inspiration from the land and have found ways to cope with the loneliness. I knew before I chose this lifestyle that I had the ability to spend a lot of time by myself. Another aspect is that I have to be disciplined. It's not hard for me to work; it's hard to know when to stop. I joined the San Francisco Design Network, which turned out to be a lot of fun. We get together once a month and I enjoy the various presentations and bouncing ideas off the other artists."

FUN AND THE ONE-PERSON BUSINESS

Few callings in life offer as great a chance to have fun as a one-person business. First, the work itself is most likely fun, so you can just linger over the parts you love most. Second, you control the pace. If you follow the tips offered in this book, you should be able to slow down and do the diverting things that catch your eye at the moment. Talk to the postmistress, watch a butterfly, play with a child you pass at the park, skip a rock across a stream . . . and spend an extra half hour getting to know a new person you met over morning coffee at the local coffee shop.

But to make this happen you must plan for it. At first it may seem contradictory to talk about planning your fun. Fun is supposed to arise spontaneously from other activities and it often does. But it is also very easy to get so involved in the day-to-day operation of your business that that's all you do. One of the most frequent complaints we hear is, "I don't ever seem to have enough time for fun!"

The solution is to build in fun. Remember to add little pieces of time onto some of your business activities so that there's room for fun as well. If it takes a half hour to go to the post office, schedule forty-five minutes so you won't feel you have to pass up an interesting conversation with a friend you happen to meet there. If you can see a heavy day coming later in the week, schedule a movie for that evening as a reward for making it through the day. This way, you will keep your spirits high, be more likely to recognize those moments when they arise, and be able to take advantage of them without worrying about your busy schedule and the demands placed on your time by your business.

"I once spent three years, having no fun in my work. The only fun was the work I was doing on my own time. Those three years of steady work were unusual for me because I had been an independent for so long. They really taught me that the most important thing is to have fun every day rather than wait for it on Friday. For me, fun is more important than making a lot of money. It's not so much just having fun as feeling that my creative energies are driving the day, not some other demands." That's how book designer and consultant Clifford Burke explains the importance of fun in his life.

He goes on to say, "The biggest risk of the one-person business is overwork. You have to avoid burying yourself in work. It's not a pleasure unless you get off on overwork, and some people do, I guess. If your life is dedicated to the business and something emotional or spiritual or physical happens to jeopardize your ability to run it, there is nothing to fall back on. Human beings are just more complex than that. You can wake up fifteen years later and not know who your kids are. It took me a long time to learn to take time, to be lazy. Having learned it, I consider it a real treasure. I still work very hard. I just treasure my time."

For many one-person businesses, the fun is intrinsic to the business itself. Teri Joe Wheeler finds fun and excitement in all aspects of her work. "It's really fun when I walk into a store with a bag of my things and it turns into an 'ooh, ahh' situation. I really adore fabric, so it's exciting to have new ones. It's fun also because if someone is happy with their bag, then it's rewarding."

Maybe the real secret to having fun in business is best expressed by Pam Glasscock, a watercolorist. "One thing that really influenced me was in college. I went to a lecture and the professor said something that really struck me. I think about it a lot. He said 'You have to figure out what you love and do that.' That's rule number one."

SUPPORT FROM FRIENDS AND COLLEAGUES

By experimenting with different systems for ourselves and observing the ways our clients and people we interviewed for this book cope with the emotional support issue, we have come up with four alternatives that work for most people: planning buddies, business support groups, advisors, and business advisory boards.

Planning Buddies

The planning buddy is an idea we were first introduced to by Barbara Sher in *Wishcraft*. Planning buddies offer each other a special kind of friendship that is unconditional. You agree to meet weekly and to serve as a catalyst for one another, but not as therapists or counselors. Your weekly agenda should have three parts:

1. Catch up on each other's activities in the preceding week. What you report may be either business-related or personal.
2. Allow each person to tell the other about any hard times—moments or events in the last week that were emotionally disruptive. This part of the meeting is not about fixing anything. The listener should just listen, and if the talker wants advice, he or she will have to ask for it. This is an important rule.
3. Tell each other what your plans are for the coming week, and use this opportunity to set a goal. The other person's job is not to punish or harass you if you don't meet your goal, but to help you put your goal outside of yourself, out into the real world. When you seriously tell someone what you want to accomplish, the chance that you will actually reach the goal increases. At the very least, you may see that the goal wasn't what you really wanted anyway.

Attorney Catherine Campbell thinks the planning buddy is the most important of all support systems. "There is a very strong series of overlapping circles that form a net that supports me in what I do and, of course, supports everybody else involved in similar kinds of work. The 'one on one' is the most important of the support systems. All the social networks in the world would not be enough if I did not have that one close friend with whom I could talk and plan."

Business Support Groups

Business support groups are especially important to one-person businesses. Individuals who are in business for themselves get together from one to four times per month. At these meetings you listen to business problems and successes, share concerns and useful information, and lend each other emotional support.

As with the planning buddy, an important value comes from getting your plans, dreams, and hard times out on the table. But the business support group differs from the planning buddy in two ways. First, because there are more people involved, you get more support. Second, business support groups tend to focus on work-related goal setting more than on emotional issues. There is more brainstorming to find solutions, and more checking in to see how well group members are accomplishing things on their to-do lists.

For instance, at one meeting you might hear, "I want you all to know that I will make four phone calls a day to my prospect list until our next meeting." And at the next meeting, that person might report back, "I did it, and I'm proud of myself—I got two new clients." Although this is a lot like the third item on the planning buddy agenda, setting a goal in front of a group seems to be even more motivating, leading to even more goal completions.

A business support group can provide emotional support just as a planning buddy can, but with an important difference: It is unfair to expect one single person whom you see every week to be always upbeat and strong emotionally. With the group, you spread the support responsibilities around, making it easier on everyone.

Advisors

There are always others who know more about some aspect of your business, or your business community, than you do. If you can identify who they are, and find that you enjoy spending time together, then you have found your advisors.

The advisor relationship is a delicate one and needs special attention. You must be careful not to overstep your welcome in asking for help. Generally an advisor should be the last person you go to, when your planning buddy or your support group has been unable to answer your question. But sometimes an advisor is the first person you go to, especially if you have a problem in the day-to-day operation of the business, and you know that one of your advisors would know the precise answer. The general rule for treatment of advisors is to respect them and to value their time as you would your own.

Business Advisory Boards

A business advisory board differs from a business support group in that it meets only as frequently as necessary and is made up of people with expertise that is valuable to your business. It might include your local banker or a loan officer from the branch where you bank; your accountant and perhaps a business lawyer; one or more of your special advisors; one or more of your suppliers; and so forth. This group is not for emotional support, although you might incidentally find a lot of emotional support, given the interest that these people have in your business. The primary purpose of an advisory board is to meet with you once or twice a year at crucial times: to help guide your business as it grows, to help you through a business crisis, or to help you find answers to business problems that you have not been able to resolve elsewhere. Your job is to do your homework, including extensive library and real life research. Then, when you convene your advisory board, you are fully prepared to answer any questions they might have about the issues surrounding your problem.

Examples of Sources of Support

Kate Bishop, a clothes designer, uses a planning buddy and networking with other designers as a source of support. "I have a situation with another designer that I enjoy a lot. We have a semiformal agreement to spend time at each other's studios about once a week. We bring whatever we're working on, or work on something together. We set challenges for each other, like homework assignments that we have to show each other at a certain time. It's really stimulating. It's also fun and we learn from each other.

"I've been doing a lot of networking with other designers. I belonged to the San Francisco Design Network for about a year and a half, and I found it real inspiring. But the Design Network wanted to be on the cutting edge of fashion, and I was sort of an outcast when I didn't do the latest look. That experience helped me define my own style better and my own needs. Now I've replaced that association with networking with designers who have the same needs and goals that I do. I call them up and say, 'I'm Kate Bishop. I've heard of you. I'd love to see your studio. Where do you get rhinestones? How do you handle this problem or that? We must have a lot of similar business problems, since we're both working by ourselves. Let's get together and talk.'

"I take single-handed responsibility for getting the designers in my area to know each other. I make an effort to get to know other designers and to share as much as I can with them."

Paul Terry, a business advisor, uses all of the emotional support methods we recommend. "Isolation is not something I can avoid. It happens to me and my clients. Ironically, it's like the wounded healer—giving advice to clients on how to deal with isolation when you yourself are dealing with the same issue. I think that's part of my strength as an advisor; often I am dealing with or have dealt with exactly what a client is going through.

"I deal with isolation by trying to involve myself in relationships that will have a positive effect on my business. I've had two or three different support partners on an ongoing basis, I've been involved in three support groups, and now belong to a support group that meets weekly. I use business advisors, people whom I call for things that I'm stuck on or need help with. Emotional and psychological needs can be met by support partners or groups if they are open enough to deal with those things. Staying in touch with friends is important too. Sometimes I have to put a lot of energy into just arranging to have breakfast or lunch with someone, or making myself go to certain events or get involved in activities that are helpful in dealing with isolation. It can be something as mundane but as fun as playing softball on a regular basis or having a tennis partner or running with somebody."

Suzanne Maxson, a job development researcher, relies mostly on friends. "I have a rich circle of friends who have kept me alive for years. Women who work and are up and down with it all the time. Recently I've developed a relationship with a woman who does what I do in a very similar situation. We've decided it would be helpful to communicate more.

"The woman who turned the business over to me is definitely a mentor and has played a big part in my life. The counselor I work with isn't an advisor, but his respect for what I do and his appreciation keep me going. Whenever I give him a lead he says, 'Nice work!' Then there is another counselor who is always there to answer questions. And that's important because when I jumped into this, I knew nothing, and she is the one I can turn to."

EMERGENCY EMOTIONAL NEEDS—PERSONAL INTERVENTION RESOURCE GROUP

Sometimes a personal emotional crisis, either in the business or in your personal life, can be so critical that it needs special attention. Forming a kind of ad hoc emergency support group, which we call the Personal Intervention Resource group, or PIR, can provide just the kind of short-term support that you need to meet these crises. The PIR is designed to nurture and aid individual efforts with the help of friends and associates.

First, it is ad hoc; it appears when you need it. It needs no maintenance when it is not in use. You call it together to meet a particular need and disband it when that need has been met. In fact the PIR doesn't work well if you try to make it an ongoing thing.

In addition, unlike a support group, the PIR has a binding, two-way nature. If you call your friends together to help you manage a personal crisis, it means you are going to take seriously what they tell you to do, and it also means that they have a responsibility to give you their absolute best.

When Do You Use a PIR?

PIRs can be helpful in getting through two life situations that occur more frequently today: the personal transition (career change, divorce, life-threatening disease, etc.) and business crises. Whatever the situation that moves you to call a PIR, be sure you are ready to accept your friends' advice and to act on it.

Phillip M., for example, was encountering clear-cut cases of theft and fraud at work. He had pointed them out to his superiors, but they had made it clear they wanted him to look the other way. He didn't know what to do. His integrity required him to stick with this problem until it was corrected, but if he did, he stood a good chance of losing his job and creating a public scandal. His PIR supported him in the best possible way. They told him to resign and then tell all that he knew to the proper authorities. Without the support of his friends, and their confirmation of his values, taking this course would have been much more difficult. And his friends knew that in making that recommendation, they would also have to be there for Phillip afterward when he was trying to continue his career on some other path.

PIRs can also be useful for less drastic life issues. Nancy M. was having trouble in controlling her spending habits. She met monthly with a group of friends to share business financial statements, and this helped her see where her money was going. Later, because she was still having difficulties with impulse buying and spending money in response to stress, she started a PIR. She got members of her PIR to form a two-person committee to act as her money governor. Whenever she felt the need to spend more than $50, she was required to call these two friends and get their agreement. Surprisingly, she never needed to call them at all. Just knowing they were there allowed her to control her spending habit.

Whom Should You Invite?

The membership of your PIR is crucial. It is important that the friends you pick for your PIR have enough of an overlap in their values to arrive at a consensus. Ralph R. invited six close friends who turned out to be incompatible. Because they had conflicting values, they couldn't agree on an appropriate action for him to take. This left Ralph without the help he needed.

How Big Should It Be?

We've seen PIR groups from one to ten. The size that works best is about four to six. More than that requires someone to act as a group facilitator to make sure that everyone gets heard and to keep track of the time. With four to six, members of the group tend to take care to hear each other, each taking responsibility to see that something comes of the meeting in the time allotted.

How Long Should It Last?

To make the PIR work most effectively, you do not want it to be a burden on your friends. But you do want them to come up with recommendations that will be meaningful to you. If they spend less than an hour you'll probably wonder how useful their advice can be to you. On the other hand, many report that nothing gets accomplished after the first two hours of a meeting, so you are left with the conclusion that a PIR should last somewhere between one and two hours.

What Structure Should You Use?

Once everybody is gathered together and ready to work on the problem, it is up to you to present the issues clearly. Make sure you provide enough background material for your advisors to understand the situation. Ask if they need more information. Make sure they understand what you want of them. Then leave. Go for a walk. Go make some phone calls, do anything, just so you let the group have time alone to speak frankly about what to recommend.

Return at the appointed hour and make a written list of the recommendations. Ask questions if anything recommended is not clear. Set a date for a follow-up meeting where you can report your progress. Then go out and do your best to implement their advice.

What Do You Do If Your PIR Doesn't Produce the Kind of Advice You Had Hoped For?

Question yourself deeply about your willingness to listen. If you're sure you are open to receiving advice from your friends, then look closer at whom you asked to be in the group. But first, re-examine the way you presented the problem. Were your friends underinformed? Did you make it clear what you wanted from them?

If you do not feel you can follow their advice, thank them for their efforts. Think it over for a few days, and then give it a try anyway. If you find it simply isn't working for you, schedule a new meeting to discuss your doubts and clear up the difficulties.

If it seems that you made a mistake in your choice of PIR members, think about it for a few days, and start over with a new group.

Once you master clarity and the art of choosing the right people, you will find the PIR to be an indispensable tool for work or life transitions and crises. If you decide to try setting up your own Personal Intervention Resource group, let us know about your successes, or your difficulties.

TIME OFF

Taking time off is not only a wonderful idea, it is also good business strategy because it promotes emotional stability. Every one-person business should build two kinds of time off into its calendar: vacations and no-agenda time.

Vacations

Vacations are among the most effective contributors to emotional stability. As tension and stress accumulate over time, a vacation that offers a complete change of setting and freedom from responsibilities can alleviate many problems. Afterward you can return to your business with a fresh perspective, full of vim and vigor.

Many people won't take vacations because their identity is so tied to their work that they can't imagine themselves without it. Ralph, a real estate financier and a workaholic, is a good example of that. Every time he plans a vacation, something at work comes up to force him to cancel. His identity is too weak for him to feel comfortable on a vacation, so work always takes precedence. He isn't alone; many people who appear to be wrapped up in their business are really just uncomfortable on their own.

Admittedly, during the first few years of starting a business there is often too much work to do and too little revenue. It may not be possible to take a vacation during this time. But the main reason one-person proprietors give for not taking vacations is that there is no way to deal with the business that comes in while they are gone. They fear that the momentum of the business will be lost and that customers will begin to view them as unreliable. There are two answers to this: One is to create and use backup support. Another is to plan something to inject new life into your business upon returning, such as a marketing event or a community party.

The function of a vacation is clear from the Latin roots of the word, *vacatio* and *vacare*, meaning to be free, to be empty. Yet the most common vacation, staying at home or near home, is also the worst possible one for building emotional stability. We call it "taking a bath with your clothes on." This is because you will not stop thinking about work or being stimulated by it unless you are well away from it.

Get far away from your work, geographically, into a different climate, different air, and different sky color. Get far away in time as well. Taking four days off to rest is a good idea, but don't call it a vacation. Your mind takes that long to stop thinking about important issues. Two weeks may be an emotional minimum; much shorter than that may not be worthwhile. In fact, too short a vacation may make matters worse if you return without the emotional renewal needed to handle the work that accumulated in your absence. Consider that it takes at least three days to get into the vacation and three more to prepare to return to the work world. So if you take only one week off, you will get only one day of real vacation.

Lastly, don't plan a vacation that is more work than what you left behind. Even if the work is different, it shouldn't be without relaxation. Property managers Ted Rabinowitsh and Diane Stuart have a prescription that works well with their type of business. "We work on a project until it gets done, starting early and ending late. But when we go on vacation, we usually go for two or three months."

Musician Alicia Bay Laurel schedules her vacations for the slow periods of her business, in May and September. "Being an entertainer in Hawaii, I'm always at work when other people are vacationing or playing. During some periods there are hardly any tourists, so sometimes I'll plan to travel off the island then and just cancel whatever work might come up, because that's when I'll take the smallest amount of loss. I have friends who live all over the country and I don't get to see them all that often so every couple of years I like to take a month or two off and go visit them."

These three elements, change of geography, enough time, and a change of pace, are each an important part of emotional renewal. If you have never had a vacation with a change of geography, at least two weeks off, and a change of pace, try it. It is hard to appreciate without having experienced it once.

No-Agenda Time

What we call no-agenda time has a magical, rejuvenating effect. With no-agenda time, you set aside part of a day, a whole day, or several days, and when you enter that time, you have one simple rule: It doesn't matter what you do as long as it isn't planned.

Claude sets aside every day ending in zero as a no-agenda day. On the 10th, 20th, and 30th he doesn't make any appointments, not even appointments with himself to get administrative work done. He gets up at his regular time, but instead of rushing out the door to his first meeting, he enjoys a leisurely breakfast and over coffee decides what he would like to do most that day. Because he enjoys his work very much, it is inevitable that sometimes he will choose to pay bills or balance the checkbook. But he may also go to the beach, or drop in on friends, go shopping for new clothes, or do whatever else meets his fancy.

A useful effect of no-agenda time is the perspective it gives you on how you feel about the rest of your time. If you wake up thinking that you really should do that report or box up those ceramic mugs that have to go out, and the overriding emotion is one of resentment, this is a warning signal you should pay attention to. Maybe you only need a vacation, but you may also need to re-examine your long-range goals.

ACTIVE HEALTH PRACTICES

Learning more about taking care of your health is a major weapon against disease and emotional turbulence. Many people's first reaction to pain is to go straight to a doctor to have the pain removed. We recommend that you pause for a moment and ask yourself a few questions: Where did this pain come from? What is going on emotionally? What have I done or eaten recently? What are the strategies that I have used in the past to handle this kind of problem? In this way you will be actively taking responsibility for your own health. The answers will tell you whether it is really necessary to go to a doctor. Moreover, taking control of the healing process will raise your self-esteem, again contributing to emotional stability.

In taking charge of your health, exercise and diet are two of the most important factors in helping to maintain emotional stability.

Exercise

The form of exercise you engage in is less important than doing it on a regular basis. You need not become a marathon runner or spend two hours a day in the gym doing aerobics or weight lifting. Something as simple as a brisk fifteen-minute walk around the block every day can be an effective way to help maintain your emotional stability. If you wish to be more physically fit, the American Col-

---

What Does Staying Fit Mean?

Opinions vary about just what constitutes base fitness and how it can be measured. Some researchers like Dr. Kenneth Cooper, founder and president of the Aerobics Center in Dallas, think fitness can be measured by a point system that's based on aerobic exercise. The Cooper baseline, promoted in various best-selling books, is 30 to 35 aerobic points scored weekly.

Others such as Stanford Medical School's Dr. Ralph Paffenbarger, who conducted a landmark study of Harvard University alumni, think in terms of the number of extra calories one burns each week while exercising. Paffenbarger's baseline is 2,000 calories.

At first glance, Cooper and Paffenbarger seem to differ. If your exercise is walking, you can please Cooper by walking four miles in less than an hour, four days a week. Those 16 miles would score 32 aerobic points. Since each mile walked burns approximately 100 calories, it seemingly would require 20 miles to satisfy Paffenbarger's standard.

But Cooper points out that Paffenbarger's study included even such background exercise as climbing stairs or walking to the bus stop in accumulating the weekly 2,000 calories. "If you compare what he says with what I say," states Cooper, "my people scoring 32 points are probably burning at least 2,000 calories." Marathon running and sweaty aerobic dance routines count, but so would mowing the lawn and being the active partner in sex. Although researchers quibble over points and calories and various other means of measuring fitness, they do agree on one thing: Many methods can be used as ways to get fit and stay fit.

There's an important benefit that both doctors agree upon. "For each hour of physical activity, you can expect to live that hour over, and one or more to boot," says Paffenbarger. Cooper notes that one of the most dramatic findings of the Paffenbarger study was that exercise could prolong the life of a middle-aged person by 24 to 30 months. "That may not seem like much," says Cooper, "until you realize that if cancer were completely eradicated in this country, our lifespans would increase by exactly the same amount."

Sweating is necessary, Paffenbarger claims, but it does not matter how hard you sweat. "You do not need bursts of energy to add years to your life," he says. "There is no benefit from vigorous sports. You don't need to run marathons. Walking is enough." He found that if you burn more than 3,500 calories, it produces no additional benefits.

The top line of Cooper's target zone is 80 points. Says Cooper, "If you exercise more than that, you're doing it for reasons other than fitness."

From Hal Higdon, "Base Fitness," *The Walking Magazine* (February/March, 1988).

lege of Sports Medicine recommends from fifteen to sixty minutes of walking, jogging, cycling, or swimming, three to five times per week as a minimum.

At the very least, take breaks and go for a walk. Part of the benefit comes from the increased circulation and exposure to sunlight. But also important is the regularity. Regularity is a very effective tool. It creates a kind of rhythm that gives you a sense of stability, even in the midst of the periodic chaos that can arise in successful businesses. Regular physical activity is also one of your best investments for health in old age.

Diet

Diet goes hand in glove with regular physical activity. As with exercise, eating meals at regular times is as important as what you eat. Having established meal regularity, you can go on to review the nutritional content of your diet. You can also promote stability by taking the time to prepare your own food. Careful preparation of meals requires planning and a different pace from that required for managing your business. It can be a rejuvenating experience to pause for an hour to prepare a meal with care and then eat it—much more so than rushing out to a restaurant or fast-food outlet. Part of the reason for being in business for yourself is to be able to set and enjoy your own pace. So think twice about letting the urgency of your business force you to eat out and gulp down a quick meal before rushing back to the fray. Don't just take our word for it. Spend one week cooking all your own meals at home, with planning and forethought. See if it doesn't provide the emotionally stabilizing effect we predict, not to mention the soothing effect it will have on your digestive system.

Insurance

If you exercise and eat regularly and sensibly, you will probably find yourself in good health, both physically and emotionally. If so, you may never need to make a claim on an insurance policy of any kind.

It is likely, therefore, that you will buy health insurance almost entirely because it will increase your emotional stability by decreasing your worry about what to do if you get sick or are in an accident. The same is true for life insurance, disability insurance, and so forth. You will evaluate all of them from the point of view of "in the unlikely event." Their main value is that you will worry less about how you would cope with a disaster or untoward event. And when you are healthy you can reduce the cost of your insurance premiums by buying policies with a large deductible amount.

CONCERNS ABOUT OLD AGE

People have many reasons for being afraid of old age, and these worries affect emotional stability. The most common fears are of physical disabilities and infirmities related to health, being a financial burden to family and friends, and being overly dependent on others for getting around.

Most people respond to these fears by saving as much money as possible. As a one-person business owner, you may be able to take a different approach, one that is not so dependent on savings, and the need to save money for that purpose might be satisfied with a more modest amount.

Calculating the savings needed to generate a desired income is simple. At age sixty-five an annuity that will pay you $250 a month for the rest of your life costs $30,000. At $40 per month it would take thirty years to save this much, including five percent interest compounded monthly. So you would have to begin by age thirty-five, or else increase your monthly savings accordingly. If you want more than $250 per month when you retire, you will have to save proportionally more.

People who own businesses need less savings for two reasons. First, if you have a business that can be sold, and most can, the best savings plan would be to invest in the business. Second, to many people, retirement is an escape from a job. But if you are already doing what you love, what is there to escape from?

The main question you should have about investing in your own business is not whether the investment will yield a high enough return, but whether you will ever get your capital back. In other words, can you someday sell your business for a good price? Although one-person businesses as we know them today are a new phenomenon, in traditional fields such as dental, medical, insurance, legal, and accounting, it has been easy to sell a good practice. The keys to getting a good price are all the points made in this book: loyal clients, good service, superb record keeping, good backup for overflow work and vacations, and a diversified customer base. So if you put your money into making the business better in these ways, in the future you'll be likely to get your capital back.

Are the concerns of a one-person business owner about old age the same as those of a salaried retiree? No! A salaried person usually has no way to earn a few extra dollars, no way to earn money in new ways in changing times or to cut costs. A salaried person is often uneasy at the prospect of a world without a steady income. Except for occasional dabbling in real estate, most salaried people have no fallback position if inflation hits or the unexpected happens.

You on the other hand have the must useful of all human skills—the ability to make money with your own resources. If you can do it now, you can always do it. Your skills as a sole proprietor will get better the longer you are in business and the older you get. You can always earn money; you can always get a business deal of some sort going. The important planning for old age is to continue to improve your business skills, diversify your business into new directions as times change, and be flexible in changing markets.

On the whole, the idea of retirement should probably seem ridiculous to you. Salaried people retire to do the things they have always dreamed of—hobbies, reading, treasure hunting, leisure, travel. But you are already doing what you dream of. That is what your business is about. And when your dreams change, you can change your business. So retirement hasn't the same meaning for you. Instead of talking about retirement, people who have their own businesses talk about learning new skills and practicing them in new parts of the world, trying out business ideas that have been on the back burner, or adding some social action to their work that is important to them.

Bill Morehouse, fine artist, says this about preparing for old age. "I will probably never retire from art. I'm not sure old age is going to slow me down. I'm not happy unless I'm investigating something or making something and just being part of the growth process that never really stops until you finally croak. So the idea of retirement and old age is a strange one for me. You just keep going until you can't do it anymore."

Eileen Mulligan, landscape gardener, knows she won't be able to continue in this line of work when she's old. "I own my own home, which is important, and I also have two children who I put a lot of juice into. If they don't take care of me when I'm an old lady, I'll come after them. I know how to grow my own food. I'm strong and healthy."

Alicia Bay Laurel, musician, also thinks of doing something different in her old age. "The other things that I have done to make a living are more appropriate for that time of my life. I write and paint and draw. I think that in old age I will be more reclusive and will spend a lot more time doing those things. I look forward to that. I look now at my art and writing projects and wonder why I don't get around to them. I know it's because I have this fire inside to get out there and play music. So when that fire is spent, which I assume will be sometime in my fifties, then I'll be able to turn my attention to these other things that have been on the back burner."

Ted Rabinowitsh, whose business is building restoration and property management, says, "What we're doing is better then anything else because we're creating something that can supply us income. I mean you build up equity so you can sell properties. We don't qualify for Social Security, Medicare, pensions, or anything, so it's completely up to us. Now we have Blue Shield, with a real high deductible." For Diane Stuart, Ted's partner, "Retirement is not a goal. I can't imagine not working on something at any given time."

Norman Prince, photographer, feels the same. "I believe that as long as I am not disabled, I will continue working as a photographer, a teacher, and a consultant, and I'll keep marketing my stock for the rest of my life. I don't intend to stop. I like a lot of my work, and I like to think that part of my future income will come from resale of my pictures for use in new editions, new books, etc. Also from future sales of pictures from my stock files through subcontractor agencies in this country and overseas. Since I've never really worked a regular job, I don't have any of the advantages of it, but I don't have any of the disadvantages either—like compulsory retirement or being forced out of business or losing my job because the company is moving or shutting down."

Social Security

Automatic saving occurs on your behalf when you pay your Social Security tax. The amount you will receive depends primarily on your earnings from age fifty to sixty-five. As of 1987, you will receive $230 a month based on average annual net earnings of $3,600. For the next $15,000 earned you will get $410, and so on. Although the limit is now around $600 a month for one person, all the proportions will increase at a steady rate when adjusted for future inflation. In the year 2011, however, the retirement age will be moved to sixty-six and twenty years later sixty-seven.

Most people are eligible for Medicare coverage even if they paid into Social Security for only one three-month quarter in their life. Through Social Security, nearly everyone is covered for major medical expenses with a plan that has a twenty percent deductible. Two drawbacks to Medicare are that it can only be used for traditional forms of medicine, which doesn't include many holistic practices, and it won't cover extraordinary needs such as traveling long distances to see a particular specialist. For such expenses you will need a savings account or a special health insurance policy.

On a positive note, medical care has been changing rapidly and is increasingly considered a fundamental human right in much of the world. This means that with every passing day it is more likely that the quality of medical care for the aged will improve and be more readily available. The lag between the introduction of new medical practices and their widespread availability is only a few years. So it is only a matter of time before today's expensive "special" treatments become tomorrow's affordable standard treatments.

Keoghs

A sole proprietor can set money aside under a Keogh Plan, which allows the savings to be deducted as an expense from your personal income and taxation to be avoided until you draw on these funds. You will supposedly pay less tax because you will be in a lower tax bracket at that time. Any financial institution, such as a bank, an insurance company, or a stockbroker, can help you set up a Keogh. The amount you can set aside is substantial.

RESOURCES

Dennis T. Jaffe and Cynthia D. Scott, *From Burnout to Balance* (New York: McGraw-Hill, 1984).

Michael Phillips, *Simple Living Investments for Old Age,* (San Francisco: Clear Glass, 1984).

David K. Reynolds, *Constructive Living* (Honolulu: University of Hawaii Press, 1984).

Barbara Sher and Annie Gottlieb, *Wishcraft: How to Get What You Really Want* (New York: Ballantine, 1983).

Ellen Y. Siegelman. *Personal Risk: Mastering Change in Love and Work* (New York: Harper & Row, 1983).

Growth

11

Staying a One-Person Business

This last chapter deals with the problems of staying a one-person business if you have large volumes of work or if you get sick or need a vacation. Because you are almost certain to find yourself in at least one of these circumstances, you need to plan referrals, build good relationships with subcontractors, find and cultivate good suppliers, and know how to use part-time employees and apprentices to good advantage. Finally, staying a one-person business also means staying current in your field.

WHY YOU NEED BACKUP

Occasionally, you just won't be able to work. You get sick or emotionally overloaded, want to take a vacation, or have to deal with a family emergency. At such times you need backup help. If your need for backup occurs because you are facing a tight deadline or an emergency, having a system already in place will help you get through.

There are two ways to plan for backup before you need it. One is to have a good referral system, and the other is to have your office systems in such good order that someone else could come in and run your business while you were away. If you have taken all the advice and words of wisdom offered in this book, your business is probably so well organized that any competent person could fill in for you.

Referrals

Referring work to others can be a touchy subject for a one-person business. Insecurity creeps in. What if the person you recommend is more appropriate for your client? What if he or she does a bad job, and not only do you lose the client but word gets around that you are not very professional?

You can do little about the first problem of losing a client except presume that you will also inherit clients from referrals. Console yourself with the thought that the change of clients would eventually have happened anyway if the match with your substitute was really more appropriate. As in any relationship, holding on isn't worth the energy if the other person isn't interested.

Most of the businesses we have worked with find that better than eighty percent of the clients they refer elsewhere in emergencies return to them. Given this figure and considering that you might lose clients anyway if you don't make referrals when you can't handle the work, you might as well take the plunge. With experience will come the confidence and knowledge that you really are the best choice for certain clients.

Nadine Travinsky, gift store operator, can turn to her husband for backup. "He knows the business and I keep everything up to date. I also have a friend who has worked for me a few times who could help in an emergency. My store is like a big baby to me, and the first time I had my friend mind it, I would pop in all the time to make sure everything was all right. Now I have confidence that she could cover for me if I needed her."

Book designer Clifford Burke finds that he increasingly needs to do referrals. "There was a time when I hated to refer anybody to anyone. I wanted to do everything! Now there are lots of things that I don't want to do. I'm realizing that I need a good referral list and I will have to go out and build one. If somebody comes to me for something that I can do and I don't have the time, finding somebody else that can do what I can do is hard. Finding somebody who can do what I can't do isn't so hard. How do you find another me?"

In computer and training consultant Bill Dale's business, other team members can take his place. "They have already done so on one occasion so that I could represent my old school in a golf tournament. My criteria for choosing other consultants to work with are that I must have firsthand knowledge of their work, they must work to a high standard, they must understand what I expect from them, and they must be capable of working with minimal supervision."

"This office works by a process that's simple and clear," states Paul Terry, small business advisor. "If someone had the skills to do business consulting, had values and philosophies similar to mine, and could use a computer, they would find it a fairly straightforward job to answer the phone, see clients, and generate information and reports. I know two or three people who could come in and do that."

For unusual businesses finding a substitute is obviously harder. Nevertheless, it is important to have a list of alternatives. Just as you appreciate it when a retail business tells you where to buy something that they don't have, so your clients will appreciate your concern for their needs.

Subcontractors

In chapter 9, Legal Matters, we talk about who is and who is not an independent contractor. This judgment is a matter of law and ruling by the IRS. Here we are going to talk about working with other people from a completely different perspective.

Subcontracting is an agreement in which you promise to pay someone else for services to you or on your behalf, or for manufacturing a product or parts of a product for you. The promise can be in writing, or it can be verbal. In business it is often verbal.

When you offer a high school student $10 to fold and stuff a pile of envelopes, you're hiring a subcontractor. When you leave a stack of pages overnight at a copy center and ask for one hundred copies each, you're hiring a subcontractor. And if you are a small publisher who hires a book distributor to fill your bookstore orders, you're hiring a subcontractor.

Those first two agreements are probably verbal and the last written. All three are bona fide contracts. And even with simple examples like these, the key to making them work is to be absolutely clear about what each party expects of the other.

The Importance of Clear Agreements Business has a long history of competition, antagonism, and mutual distrust among participants. And even if you and we are not part of this picture, it still needs to be faced. Clear agreements offer the best way of avoiding unpleasantness and of having open, honest relations with people. And the best way to keep the agreements clear over time is to write them down.

Drafting a written agreement reminds you to consider all the dimensions of the agreement, be it a single transaction or an ongoing relationship, and to make sure that both parties genuinely understand what is expected. Most of all, a well-written agreement, complete with a mediation clause, provides a simple, unemotional remedy for the countless little things that can go wrong.

A written agreement is a contract and as such should always contain certain basic elements. The most important part of any contract is the mediation or arbitration clause. We recommend including a list of friends and associates who have agreed to participate as mediators or arbitrators should you have a disagreement. This is effective because by showing the contract to several people in your community, you have made your agreement public. Making the agreement public has two advantages: You will make sure that it is a good agreement before you sign it, and you will be less likely to succumb to the all-too-human tendency to remember past agreements in your favor. Of the many agreements we have seen that were submitted to potential mediators before they were signed, not one has gone to mediation after it took effect.

The next most important part of an agreement is a statement of the personal reasons for engaging in the agreement. Don't list the profit motive here, but rather why you enjoy working together, that you hold the same values, want to achieve the same results, and so forth. This element is important because it reminds you later, if you are having difficulty with each other, why you entered into this agreement in the first place.

The other parts of an agreement are fairly standard and include explanations of how things will be done, how much money people will get, and how many of what will be delivered by when.

When to Use Subcontractors The two major reasons for using subcontractors are overflow work and project work. Project work can be any service or product venture that has many parts to it. You hire subcontractors for project work when you want people with special expertise to complete some of the parts.

Overflow Work Subcontractors come in handy when you have more work than you can do, or when you begin to get clients that you would rather pass on. If you pass work on without putting yourself in a position to supervise or review it, it is best to put the subcontractor in direct contact with the client and take a brokerage fee where reasonable.

Book designer Clifford Burke describes the most sensible approach to using a subcontractor when you don't want the work for yourself. "I try to find a subcontractor and hire him or her out through the person who will actually be paying him. So I don't take a cut. I prefer not to handle other people's money. If you want to make money off other people's money, then you have to handle it in order to strip a little away as it goes by."

Landscape gardener Eileen Mulligan agrees. "I subcontract out if something comes up that I'm not really good at. I'll find a person to do it and then put them in direct contact with the client. I prefer for them to relate directly rather than for me to be in the middle."

In some overflow situations, however, you may want to maintain control of the work, perhaps even asking your subcontractor to bill or submit sales invoices through you. In these cases you should review the work for quality and completeness as the project proceeds. Remember to allow time for the reviews and for any necessary corrections so that you can keep your promise to meet the client's needs by a certain date.

Fig. 11.1   Independent Contractor Agreement

INDEPENDENT CONTRACTOR AGREEMENT

This agreement is entered into and effective as of September 15, 1988 by Claude Whitmyer and Gail Grimes.

Claude Whitmyer and Gail Grimes wish to enter into an independent contractor relationship as follows:

PERSONAL

Claude: I am presently developing contract technical writing as a part of my consulting practice. I wish to engage in this kind of work with those who are already experienced and can lead me through it in a mentoring capacity. Gail is a top-notch motivational writer in the fund-raising arena, so I am anxious to work with her as much as possible in order to learn this type of writing.

Gail: My consulting practice is growing and I need more independent contractors who can create the same caliber work as I provide for my clients on an every-day basis. I know that with a minimum of instruction and feedback that Claude can do this kind of work. I look forward to developing an ongoing sub-contractor relationship with him.

HOW IT WORKS

Working on a project-by-project basis, Claude will do contract writing for Gail. Gail and Claude will draft an agreement before the onset of each project covering goals, objectives and deliverables, time schedule, and any particulars specific to the project. Gail and Claude will review ongoing work every thirty days, at which time Gail will give a verbal evaluation of Claude's work. Changes may be made at any time by mutual consent. This agreement shall continue for ninety days. Either party may terminate this agreement with thirty days notice to the other, in writing.

Payment will be handled in the following way:

$50.00 per hour unless otherwise agreed.

Fig. 11.1   Independent Contractor Agreement (*continued*)

GOALS AND EXPECTATIONS

Claude: My goal is to provide a quality first draft writing product, while learning to improve my technical skills in the arena of motivational writing for fund-raising. In the interest of this goal, I would like to receive more detailed feedback about my work product than might ordinarily be extended to a sub-contractor.

I expect Gail to clearly communicate assignments and deadlines. I will set my own work schedule and work in my own office space, in order to complete the assignments and meet Gail's deadlines.

Gail will be responsible for all client contact, and will provide me with enough background information to do the job. She will be available by phone during the writing process to answer questions and provide client contact should I need it.

Gail: For each project, I expect Claude to study the background material I provide and write a first draft as I specify. Claude will provide me with a type-written or computer printed copy of his work, as well as an electronic copy on media and in a format that I can use with my IBM PC and Multimate word-processing package.

Claude will make no effort to contact my clients directly, as a part of this work, and he will relinquish any public recognition of the work product done. This is "work for hire" and ownership of the work product is entirely mine.

MEDIATION

If we disagree on any matter regarding the terms of this relationship we will each choose one person from the following list, or any other person we wish, to choose a third person and mediate our disagreement. The recommendation of this team of three shall be binding.

_____   _____
Claude Whitmyer   Gail Grimes

_____   _____
Date   Date

MEDIATORS

Paul Terry
Ben Tong
Salli Rasberry
Tom Hargadon
Jill Alexander

Project Work If you are a small book publisher, you might hire one person to design your book layouts and covers, another to do all your typesetting, and another to do the printing and bindery work. If you are a market researcher, you might contract with a recruitment agency to locate your subjects, a special facility to provide space for holding your focus groups, independent focus group moderators to lead the groups, and a video crew to tape the sessions. All of these are examples of project work.

Written contracts are especially useful for project work because they help explain what you need. When a need recurs, you can review the previous agreement, and it will help you judge what worked and what didn't.

Avoid becoming too dependent on one person or one business to meet your subcontracting needs. If that person or business unexpectedly has a problem, you will have one too. For example, suppose you have been using the same mail-order fulfillment house to handle your address list and the mailing of your product for several years. A week before your next big mailing must go out, you find out that the owner has left for Peru, the operation is in chaos, and nobody knows where your client list is. This could be a big problem. The best safeguard against sudden changes in the quality or availability of work from subcontractors is to try alternative helpers from time to time, and rotate your work among the good ones.

Some Simple Rules for Subcontracting

1. Where possible use a written contract. (See the Nolo Press book, *Make Your Own Contract*, which has sample forms for almost every business arrangement imaginable.) Many people feel uncomfortable about written contracts. They fear that insisting on a written contract indicates a lack of trust. Actually, a written contract has nothing to do with trust. It would be absurd to use a subcontractor you didn't completely trust, whether you had a written contract or not. A contract won't make an untrustworthy person be trustworthy. In the end, you would be left with either a court battle or a feeling of great disappointment.
   The purpose of a written contract is to make as clear as possible what you want and what the subcontractor is expected to do. By clarifying all aspects of the work, you will avoid errors, confusion, forgetfulness, and recriminations, even among friends.
2. When dealing with a written contract, always read it. And read it carefully enough to spot anything that could go wrong.
3. Be prepared to routinely pay more to your subcontractors for the extra attention that you will always need as a one-person business: faster service, emergency or overtime work, or priority.
4. Always pay promptly. Never dawdle with your supplier and subcontractor invoices if you want to continue to get the best from them.
5. Always reward good work, not just with pay, but with imagination, personal concern, and appreciation. When a printer does a flier for you faster

than you expect, or prints twenty percent extra as a kind gesture, it is common to just say thanks and take it for granted. But for a one-person business, any extra service needs to be recognized and rewarded, even in circumstances where it doesn't mean anything to you at the moment. Michael uses a printer who loves opera and esoteric books, so Michael is always on the lookout for such books. As a result of Michael's personal interest, the printer often goes out of his way to produce better than ordinary work, or to produce it faster than usual.

6. Don't ask for exclusivity. Many businesspeople are very possessive about their work. Exclusivity is usually aimed at keeping other businesses from taking away your clients, or at keeping the competition from finding out your special way of doing things. This looks logical on the surface, but the effect is just the opposite in almost every instance. You lose touch with your market, and sooner or later you lose clients.

Computer and training consultant Bill Dale relies on informal contracts in the form of a written letter or proposal to his clients. He makes some very good points about the process of creating a contract. "Detailed contracts are more trouble than they're worth, in my experience. I recommend trying the following instead:

- Meet to review needs.
- Develop an outline showing how you could meet needs.
- Agree that the outline is okay in principle.
- Confirm the needs, methods, and agreement in writing, including a detailed financial section giving your work effort, your fees, and the return on investment to the client.
- Follow up the letter on the phone. If it is fine, go ahead on this basis; if not, determine what is needed and amend the agreement if you can. If you can't, find some other project.

"Beware of selling a client on your services if there is no real need or if they do not recognize the need. You will spend all your time justifying the project, even when it is successful. Also, don't undertake projects that are not in the client's interests, even if they want you to. Think carefully before committing to something, and then *keep your word.*"

Business advisor Paul Terry's approach is even less formal, but still relies on most of the same steps. "I used to have no contract situation at all. Now I do a verbal contract over the phone. Then I send them a basic terms and conditions page which tells them who I am, what I do, who I've done it for, what I charge, what time they have to be here, what charges will be involved, and so on. It's very clearly marked, and I make sure that they have either received it in advance of coming to the office or read it when they come. So there is a verbal understanding, a contractual relationship in the sense that they have received something and have agreed to the terms. Sometimes if the issue is more complicated, or if I'm dealing with a larger client, I write them a contractual kind of letter saying, 'Based on our conversation, it is my understanding that this is the work that we plan to do together,' etc. They may sign it and send it back, or not. The larger the client and the more complicated the issue, the more likely that we will need something in writing before the work gets done."

Part-Time People

Sometimes it is necessary to hire a part-time worker instead of a subcontractor. There are two reasons you might do this. One is that the extra work you have, which requires additional help, is of an uncertain nature. The other is that you use the part-time position to train a subcontractor.

It's hard to know how to respond to a work overflow which may or may not be a permanent increase in your work load or volume of business. One response to an unexpected increase is to work longer hours to handle it and try to maintain this pace long enough to know whether the situation is temporary. This situation is quite different from that of people who know they will have an extra seasonal load, say before Christmas, New Year's, or tax return time, and can prepare themselves.

As an example, consider a refrigerator repair woman who normally has three to five customers a day but suddenly finds herself dealing with six to eight, which keeps her working until 7:00 P.M. and all day Saturday. She doesn't know whether this is a temporary blip in business or a real increase that will continue because she is finally getting known. If this level of work continues for some time and exhaustion sets in, she will know she has to figure out an alternative. If the work does let up, and she goes back to three to five customers a day, she has worked hard and saved herself the agony of training and supervising another person for the extra business that has now evaporated.

An increased work load that turns out to be permanent can be an important crossroads in a one-person business. You will be faced with having to make a few choices. One option is to turn customers away, either by referring those you don't want to someone else, or by asking them to wait until you can get to them. In some businesses people can wait, in others they can't.

A second option is to become much more efficient so that you can handle the increase in business. This can be done in a wide range of ways, one of which is to make your operating subsystems more effective, including your use of time. Another is to find ways for clients to do more of the work themselves so that you need do only the part that you are best at. For example, your incoming telephone tape for new and inquiring prospects can list five of the most common problems your clients have and explain how to handle them. This tactic can eliminate many wasted phone calls and client visits. Another possibility is to mail customers a checklist of the information you need in order to work more efficiently, before they come to see you. However, until you can determine whether the extra work is permanent—and whether you want it—you may decide to hire a part-time person to help out.

The obvious and probably best source of temporary workers is from a temporary employment agency. Using an agency has three big advantages: First, there is no ambiguity in the employee's mind or in yours that the relationship is temporary, so there will be no problem when you no longer need the help. Second, you don't have to concern yourself with employee benefits (which are handled by the temporary agency). Third, you can get a well-qualified person without going through classified employment listings, personnel interviews, or long delays. If one temporary person doesn't meet your specifications, merely phone the agency and request someone else. Using a temporary employment agency has one other advantage. If the expense of hiring the temporary helper turns out to be more than $600, you won't have to file a 1099 form at the end of the year (which you would have had to do if you had hired the employee directly). Because your helper works for the agency, the IRS won't question whether he or she is an independent contractor. Temporary employment agency personnel may be more expensive than a person you hire on your own, but the extra cost is nearly always worth it to avoid the myriad of problems associated with being an employer.

If there are no temporary employment agencies in your area or if we haven't convinced you to rely on them, at least be aware of the three risks you face by hiring a part-time employee:

- You may become accustomed to having an employee, especially if the first person you hire is good. Then you will no longer have the benefits of a one-person business.
- During the period you have a part-time employee, you will have to act like an employer, which will take work time that you thought you were saving. You will need to do income tax withholding and tax filing on your temporary employee. If you hire an immigrant, you will have to comply with Immigration and Naturalization Service requirements, including filling out an I-9 form.
- Part-time employees can rapidly come to depend on you and fool themselves into believing that the job is permanent. Then when the work runs out, you have the miserable job of letting them go.

You can do two things to avoid the last problem. First, hire someone who can't possibly become a permanent employee. A teacher who is on vacation, a pregnant woman who intends to be a full-time mother, a neighbor's relative who is visiting for a short time, a student on summer vacation, or an airline employee with short stopovers in your town. Second, write an employment contract that clearly lays out the situation.

It is not enough simply to have employees sign such a contract. You must also make a point of meeting with them as agreed in the contract and review with them how much longer you will need them. This discipline is a courtesy to them, and it also helps you keep uppermost in your mind that the job is temporary, created to give you time to figure out whether an increased volume of work is permanent or not.

Fig. 11.2   Temporary Employment Contract

Temporary Employment Contract

Temporary Employee	Employer

Address	Address

References:

Person to Phone	Phone#	Person to Phone	Phone#

Person to Phone	Phone#	Person to Phone	Phone#

Person to Phone	Phone#	Person to Phone	Phone#

- -

I, _____, accept employment from

_____ with full recognition
that this work is of a temporary nature.

My pay will be $ _____ before taxes

and withholding, and my net take home pay at _____ (intervals)

will be $ _____ .

My employer, _____, will review with me every (day or week) the amount of work remaining to be done and give me a reliable estimate of my expected tenure, so that I will be able to plan other work or activities on my own behalf.

I agree to let my employer, _____, know with reasonable advance notice when I have other commitments that will impinge on my availability to work.

I am aware that I receive no benefits, such as vacation pay, private retirement pay, health coverage, during my employment.

Employee	Employer

Date	Date

THE PERILS OF MANAGING OTHERS

Managing other people adds a significant complication to the business that makes it much more difficult to run. Even one additional person is a major increase in complexity. It changes you from being your own boss into being a manager, which is an additional skill that you may not have. Once you become a manager, you will have the same state of mind for managing one person or five. Your freedom of movement and financial flexibility will be severely restricted.

Alexandra Hart started Folkwear Patterns with two other people. "I liked the creative process of working with others. In the course of a year, however, we went from a very low capitalized business to a concern with an international product. Our product was in *People* magazine and *Women's Wear Daily.* Letters came in from all over the world. At one point we had 30 employees. Near the end I could no longer do any creative and design work; instead I was a businesswoman responsible for all these other people." Alexandra decided to become a one-person desktop publisher, which allows her to use her impressive talent as a designer.

Kate Bishop's story is more complicated. "When I was manufacturing I had nine employees. When I realized it wasn't working very well for me financially—everybody was making a living except me—I just laid everybody off. Then people started calling me up looking for dresses they hadn't seen in the stores lately. I would make appointments to see them and eventually these commissions turned into my custom business. I'm doing a lot better now by myself.

"Employees have to be paid once a week, which is a headache. I sold my goods on net 30 day terms. People usually paid me in 60 days if I was lucky, and sometimes not at all. So there was always a cash flow problem. The financial statement looked good, but there was never enough money. I always paid my employees but sometimes that meant I didn't get my draw. It was always a source of anxiety.

"For each employee there is waste. With two employees there is twice as much. Once I started taking on more of the responsibility, I realized that some of our standard methods were geared to making a perfect product. But not necessarily economically. The people who developed the methods weren't paying the bills. I found I could cut an awful lot of corners. When I sat down at the sewing machine to produce a garment, one that took three and a half hours on the books, it took me two hours and forty-five minutes. I also found that I could get a lot more yardage out of a bolt of silk when I was cutting it myself because I'm the one paying for it. And instead of abandoning garments that had a mistake, I would just correct them. When I went through my scrap boxes after a year of working by myself, I found literally hundreds of garments worth of scraps!

"Because of all the federal regulations and employee taxes and benefits and all, if you eliminate employees you cut your overhead way down. When I had employees it took a lot of work just to keep them all busy. I had to plan and organize so that everybody could have something to do when they arrived at work. In order to get to a point where I could make money and pay my employees, I had to produce about $50,000 a month. This meant more employees, a bigger facility, bigger debts. I decided to get smaller, and it's worked out wonderfully for me."

Running a one-person business is a luxury that you shouldn't give up lightly. If you are ever tempted to hire an employee, it's important that you carefully consider the downside. With employees, you have to put a goodly amount of time into supervision and associated record keeping. Remember that the one-person business has the strategic advantage of lower overhead and no employees to manage—meaning it is easier to start and maintain your business.

If you are on the verge of bringing in an employee to help with the business, remember this litany of ten reasons for not doing so.

TEN REASONS NOT TO HIRE AN EMPLOYEE

1. *Loss of emotional freedom.* When you hire an employee, you add a whole new dimension to your own work. Now you must concern yourself with making sure that your employee's job is both interesting and meaningful. You may find yourself thinking about this dilemma late at night and into the wee morning hours.

2. *Administrative responsibility.* Not only must you concern yourself with creating an interesting job for your employee, you must also plan his or her work load to maximize output and minimize cost. Usually, simple general instructions only work for the most mundane tasks. Giving good instructions for more complex tasks—the kind that would leave you free to work on other projects—requires careful thought. Which brings us back to reason number one.

3. *Financial responsibility.* The responsibility of regularly paying someone else to work for you can become a horrible burden. You must figure out how to maintain an even, stable work flow so that you can provide the steady source of income needed to pay your employee. As a single person, you can roll with the fluctuations in work, perhaps even taking advantage of slow periods to take time off or do neglected self-development work. With an employee, you must make sure that regular income is there to make the regular paycheck.

4. *Less time off.* As pointed out in 3, gone are the days when you could use slow business periods to relax, take vacations, catch up on backlogged work, or learn new skills. You must now spend that time keeping enough work going to pay your employee, or supervising what your employee is doing. With an employee you may have to eat into savings, drum up more work than you would need just to support yourself, and live with the anxiety that doing this might cause you.

5. *The delegating work blues.* In theory, delegating sounds like a good thing. In practice, it is often more difficult than it sounds. When you give

someone else work, you have to figure out how to measure whether the work is being performed completely and correctly. Because another person isn't you, and doesn't think or do things the way you do, you might experience a nagging feeling of doubt and anxiety creeping in as you start noticing little signs that your employee might be making mistakes.

6. *Wasted time.* Not only do you have to recruit an employee, you have to do the training too. If he or she leaves before a year, the chances are pretty high that you have wasted your time. The value of the time you spent getting a new employee to the point of productivity is almost always much higher than the added productivity you received from your employee in the first year.

7. *You are on trial as a good example.* To expect an employee to do good work, you have to set a good example by constantly working hard. This forces you to give up the greatest advantage of a one-person business: flexible time. If you decide to spend the morning reading back issues of trade journals or taking a walk in the park, what do you think the employee is going to conclude about working habits? With an employee, being able to goof off from time to time or to set your own schedule could become a thing of the past.

8. *Wrong pace.* From the first day of hiring an employee, you have to give up your own pace for the employee's pace. You can't expect the employee to come in at 5:00 A.M. just because that is when you are most productive. You must now schedule your work in a more normal way. Soon you will be asking yourself: Didn't I start this business to escape the 9-to-5 pace?

9. *Quality control.* If someone else works for you, you have to make sure that everything is right before a client sees it. This makes a lot more work but you can't afford not to do it. You must develop systems and procedures to assure that only the highest quality work or product ever reaches your customers or clients.

10. *Profits.* The greatest profitability in business comes from maintaining a low overhead and keeping costs down. A highly talented one-person business owner working cooperatively with others as subcontractors can handle large or complex jobs far more efficiently than a comparable number of employees. And have more fun earning more money doing it.

You should not conclude from these downside arguments that employees are never the right choice. But when the moment comes to decide if employees are the right next step, you must be prepared to give the extra effort it takes to make a business with employees work. You must be prepared to give up many of the advantages offered by the simple one-person business form, and you must have managerial skills.

SUPPLIERS—SOME OF YOUR BEST FRIENDS

Suppliers are one of the most important resources you have. We use the word *suppliers* to include all of the people and businesses that supply you with goods and services. This means accountants, lawyers, landlords, the post office, copier technicians, gardeners, and the utility company, in addition to the manufacturers, distributors, or retailers that provide you with the products that you resell.

Relying on your suppliers as a key source of information is a wise strategy. If you need to know what package to put your product in, ask a box manufacturer. How should a newsletter be laid out? Ask your printer. Most suppliers are willing to provide you with information, especially if they feel it will lead to repeat business for them.

One-person businesses are especially dependent on suppliers for several reasons. One is that bigger businesses can often afford to keep a larger inventory of supplies and materials on hand than you can, and they can more easily survive a supplier problem, argument, or strike if necessary. Another is that your business frequently offers qualitatively better service, which if translated means faster, more flexible, and more tailored service. You need the same characteristics in your suppliers.

Consider whether the prospective supplier will be able to develop a personable and friendly relationship with you, preferably a long-term one. Will you be an important client to the supplier, based on your average volume of business over a year, or for some other reason? Will you be important enough for them to do a little extra? Weigh a quick response to your needs and greater flexibility against physical inconvenience and higher price. For most one-person businesses it is preferable to drive an extra ten minutes to pick something up and to pay full retail price if they can meet these criteria. You gain longer evening or weekend hours in exchange for quick response time and quality work the first time around.

Creating good supplier relationships is something that satchel designer Teri Joe Wheeler has thought a lot about. "I want the best raw materials possible with the shortest delivery time. My hardware, buttons, and so on come mostly from overseas and can take up to six weeks to arrive. It's a lot easier when I can just call an 800 number and my material arrives the following week. I pay my suppliers immediately, as if it was COD. In getting to know the people behind the supplies, I have settled into doing business with people I like. I also am open to other sources. I have four accounts for fabric, and three for hardware. And I still shop around.

"I stay in touch with my suppliers and try to communicate to them that I appreciate what they do. I relate to them on a people level, which makes it more fun for me, and for them, I hope."

Clothes designer Kate Bishop uses a similar approach. "I do all my research by phone now. In the early years, I spent a lot of time driving around or flying around locating suppliers. Because silk is not produced in this country, you have to deal with what few importers there are. I have found the five or six that are the best for me, where salespeople are easy to work with. This is almost more important than what they have to offer.

"At one point, my customers were slow in paying, and I got into trouble with my suppliers. I kept communicating with them, though, and they were really generous. I don't know why. At one point, I owed $15,000. That took me a year and a half to pay off, and they still do business with me. If I buy net 30 now, I try to pay it immediately. I pretend that it's COD and send a check out as soon as the invoice comes."

Gift retailer Nadine Travinsky deals with many different suppliers in order to keep her little shop well stocked. She too feels it is important to pay promptly and treat suppliers well. "I have all open accounts, net 30 days, and I always pay the full amount. I never pay the minimum. The suppliers are very good to me because of that, I think. When they come in, I always give them a sample of taffy and that seems to please them. I am always nice. A lot of store owners don't treat their sales reps very well. That's a mistake because you need a good relationship with your suppliers. I use maybe twenty suppliers at various times of the year. After a while, you learn who gives you just what you ask for. Some suppliers will stick things into your order that you didn't really want in the first place. If they keep doing it, even after you tell them about it, you stop dealing with them. In the gift business there are lots of places to buy from."

Landscape gardener Eileen Mulligan focuses on information and service as the major criteria for choosing a supplier. She too thinks good relationships are important. "I go to Harmony Farm Supply in Graton, California, because they have the best information I know of, and they have good quality stuff. It's more expensive than going somewhere else, but the service is wonderful. Otherwise, I go wherever the plants and prices are good and I have a nice personable relationship with the salespeople."

And finally, a word from mail-order publisher Bear Kamaroff. "I think the United Parcel Service is the world's greatest invention for small businesses. They are more expensive than the post office, but they are more reliable, and faster, and they will come up to my house in Laytonville. And they will come up any day that I call. I'm not big on big corporations, but I love my UPS driver—he's the nicest man I've ever met.

"The fact that I pay my bills in five days instead of thirty makes every one of my vendors love me and trust me completely. They are happy to do business with me because they know I pay my bills. Some of them give discounts for early payment. If you have large bills, it never hurts to ask if your vendor will give you a discount for early payment. With one supplier, I save $300 just for writing a check ten days early."

APPRENTICES

If you can find someone who is well matched to you and interested in learning some of what you know, you can not only contribute a great deal to this person's life and the betterment of your community, but you can also send this person out into the world as a living representative of your business.

Hal Howard, a floor finisher, has trained dozens of apprentices in the last twenty years. His community regards him as a master at floor refinishing because of the high quality work that his former students continue to do. As a result, instead of creating an army of competitors, he has created a large group of loyal supporters, and he has more work than he can handle. His former students get much of his overflow work, so it is a mutually beneficial situation.

In San Francisco, an organization called the Apprentice Alliance has been matching apprentices with small business masters since 1983. For a one-person business, taking on an apprentice can be an excellent way of getting part-time help in exchange for sharing what you know about your particular field. Here are some typical comments from masters in the Apprentice Alliance:

"The apprentice and I clicked, and the apprentice and gardening clicked. We were very straightforward with one another about our wants and needs. And we were both flexible about schedules. The work was held back at critical times by the need to explain and supervise, and by the slower pace of a nonpaid person, especially while learning. We developed a friendship and had a common interest and caring about plants. The apprentice was willing to do quality work. All in all, the match was excellent and of lasting value. The only improvement I could recommend would be on my part, to decrease my work load so there would be more leisurely periods for better training."

"I had an excellent apprentice in nonprofit management. She was willing to learn, share, and work independently. She has helped to make the operation more streamlined. I helped her to gain skills and she put her skills to use for the organization. It was a mutual-gain situation. She was treated as a very trusted and responsible member of the staff."

STAYING CURRENT IN YOUR FIELD

Most service industries offer an abundance of regular seminars and classes for those in the field. Product industries have trade shows where wholesalers present their wares to retailers and the public. When you find such offerings in your field, we encourage you to go to as many as you can.

Seminars, classes, and trade shows in general are good places to meet your peers and learn from them. People with experience in your field are often happy to give you valuable tips and answer operational questions. In most fields people in their first year could handle three times the volume with the same effort if they possessed the knowledge of someone with six years' experience.

From a marketing point of view, your peers can refer their overflow business to you, if they know and respect you. Conversely, you may meet new people entering your field or others who can handle your overflow or act as backup.

These reasons for attending professional or trade meetings are additional to the technical information you may gain. Being in the company of people who share common interests while you learn new aspects of your field is a useful diversion from your day-to-day operations.

Trade shows present a similar opportunity for making contacts and acquiring information, but they also offer a powerful sales opportunity. In most business fields, trade shows seem to work well for the selling participants.

Lastly, staying current on developments in your field can give you the confidence to teach classes and seminars yourself. This is a prime source of new business, and a potential forum for gaining the respect of your peers. It also exerts a subtle pressure to keep yourself current in your chosen livelihood.

Self-care advocate Tom Ferguson stays current by reading a lot and talking to people. "I subscribe to a lot of magazines, journals, and newsletters. I have maybe a twenty-five or thirty-five percent turnover per year in my information sources. I'm always stopping some and starting new ones. I go to the library pretty often. Also I go to meetings and trade shows because that's a good way of meeting people and keeping up on what's new."

Book designer Clifford Burke says, "I read journals as necessary, and I stay good friends with a computer nut. I'm teaching him typography so he can produce more books in the future, and in exchange, he passes on information to me.

"In terms of selling one's own talent, I operate on the rule that I don't turn down opportunity. Part of that strategy is going to new things to find opportunities. I did a seminar recently, and as it worked out, it didn't actually cost me money but I didn't get paid either. The pay came in new contacts and new offers of work. Hopefully, these will lead to more work. While manufacturers work on accrual of capital and inventory, freelancers work on accrual of recognition and connections."

Mail-order publisher Bear Kamaroff keeps an open channel to the outside world. "Once a year I try to go to the American Booksellers Association convention, which is a big get-together. I hang out for two and a half days with all the people in the book world and hobnob and shoot the breeze with them—say hello to all the wholesalers, the other small book publishers, bookstore owners I know, and the graphic artists.

"I subscribe to a lot of business and publishing publications that are applicable to me, and I skim them all. I also subscribe to a bunch of tax publications so I can keep up with the tax laws.

"Whenever I'm around people involved in business and books, I keep my ears open to hear what they have to say. I'm always open to ideas and suggestions. It's so easy to expand your business if you have time to do it. And it's so easy to just keep exploring and looking for new avenues, especially in mail order. I'm sure I could double my business if I just sat down and took the time to do it. But I don't want to take that time for my business right now. Some people feel that if you're not growing you're dying, but I don't agree with that. As long as you stay on top of things, there is no reason to keep growing unless you want to or need to."

Computer and training consultant Bill Dale reads to stay up to date and belongs to a couple of professional associations. "I am a member of the Institute of Marketing and of the Institute of Directors. I myself run many courses each year, as well as developing new ones. This keeps me fresh, as does working with clients who are involved with the fast-changing computer business."

RESOURCE

Stephen Elias, *Make Your Own Contract* (Berkeley, California: Nolo Press, 1986).

Appendix

Business Start-Up Basics

While this book is intended primarily for ongoing businesses, we would be remiss in our responsibility to those of you who are not yet in business, but who think you might like to be, if we didn't at least mention the steps necessary to starting up a business. So here is a list of what to do if you decide to take the plunge:

1. Do your market research.
2. Create a business plan.
3. Obtain the necessary licenses and permits.
4. Register your fictitious name.
5. Register to pay sales taxes.
6. Open a business bank account.
7. Hire your subcontractors.
8. Develop and execute your marketing plan.

DO YOUR MARKET RESEARCH

The very first thing to do after you come up with a new business idea is to find out how feasible it will be. In addition to verifying the availability of the raw materials to make your product or finished products to sell, you must also determine the need or desire for your products or services. This is called a market survey. A market survey tells you how many potential customers or clients of your products or services there are in the market you would like to focus on, and what the likelihood of their buying from you might be. (See chapter 8, Marketing, for more on market surveys.)

CREATE A BUSINESS PLAN

Here are the six basic steps to take in the creation of your business plan.

1. Do a market survey. This is the step we just discussed.
2. Create a statement of projected income. Determine the profit you need to cover the income you want to make, as well as the return you expect for any capital you have invested.
3. Prepare an "opening day" balance sheet. This will include a list of equipment and assets, as well as the money spent to get to opening day that can be directly attributed to the business.
4. Find the appropriate location and prepare a plan for how the space will be laid out.
5. Establish an appropriate system for keeping accounting and bookkeeping records.
6. Develop your marketing and/or merchandising plan. How will you display, promote, and sell your products or services?

OBTAIN LICENSES AND PERMITS, REGISTER YOUR FICTITIOUS NAME, REGISTER TO PAY SALES TAX

Each of these has a section of its own in chapter 9, Legal Matters.

OPEN A BUSINESS BANK ACCOUNT

It is highly desirable to have a separate checking account for your business. This will help you track income and expenses that are only related to the business.

HIRE YOUR SUBCONTRACTORS

Locate the subcontractors that you intend to use, if any, and negotiate your working relationship. Get all agreements in writing. See chapters 9, Legal Matters, and 11, Staying a One-Person Business, for help on this.

DEVELOP AND EXECUTE YOUR MARKETING PLAN

This is covered in chapter 8, Marketing.

RESOURCES

Mike P. McKeever, *Start-Up Money: How to Finance Your New Small Business* (Berkeley, California: Nolo Press, 1987).

Small Business Administration, *Business Plan For Retailers* (Publication No. 150).

Small Business Administration, *Business Plan For Small Manufacturers* (Publication No. 218).

Index

More help for the small businessperson

Second Coming of the Woolly Mammoth: An Entrepreneur's Bible by Ted S. Frost

"Bible is a fitting description. Frost's book has everything from (many more than) 10 commandments to parables offering guidelines on subjects from goals and travel to employees and sex. . . . he offers sound and practical advice for dealing with bankers, money, and financing."—*Entrepreneur* magazine $11.95 paper, 256 pages

The Small Business Test by Colin Ingram

A series of tests, based on detailed analysis of close to 100 small businesses, which allow would-be entrepreneurs to evaluate their strengths and weaknesses and greatly improve their chances of success. $8.95 paper, 96 pages

Mail Order Moonlighting by Cecil C. Hoge, Sr.

"The authoritative and best up-to-date word for anyone in the mail order business."—*The Next Whole Earth Catalog.* Everything you need to set up and run a successful mail order business, with little or no risk, from your own home. $9.95 paper, 416 pages

Working Together by Frank and Sharan Barnett

How couples can effectively work together as entrepreneurs. "The Barnetts weave the insights of 25 other entrepreneurial couples . . . into sound advice of their own. *Working Together* is sensible and inspiring."—*The New York Times* $9.95 paper or $15.95 cloth, 256 pages

Making $70,000+ a Year as a Self-Employed Manufacturer's Representative by Leigh and Sureleigh Silliphant

Be your own boss, travel as much or as little as you want, and make almost unlimited amounts of money. $9.95 paper, 224 pages

Available from your local bookstore, or order direct from the publisher. Please include $1.25 shipping & handling for the first book, and 50 cents for each additional book. California residents include local sales tax. Write for our free complete catalog of over 400 books and tapes.

Ship to:

Name _____

Address _____

City _____ State _____ Zip _____

Phone: (_____) _____

Ten Speed Press
P.O. Box 7123
Berkeley, CA 94707
For VISA or Mastercard orders call (510) 845-8414